MACMILLAN CULTURAL READERS

PRE-INTERMEDIATE LEVEL

RACHEL BLADON

# England

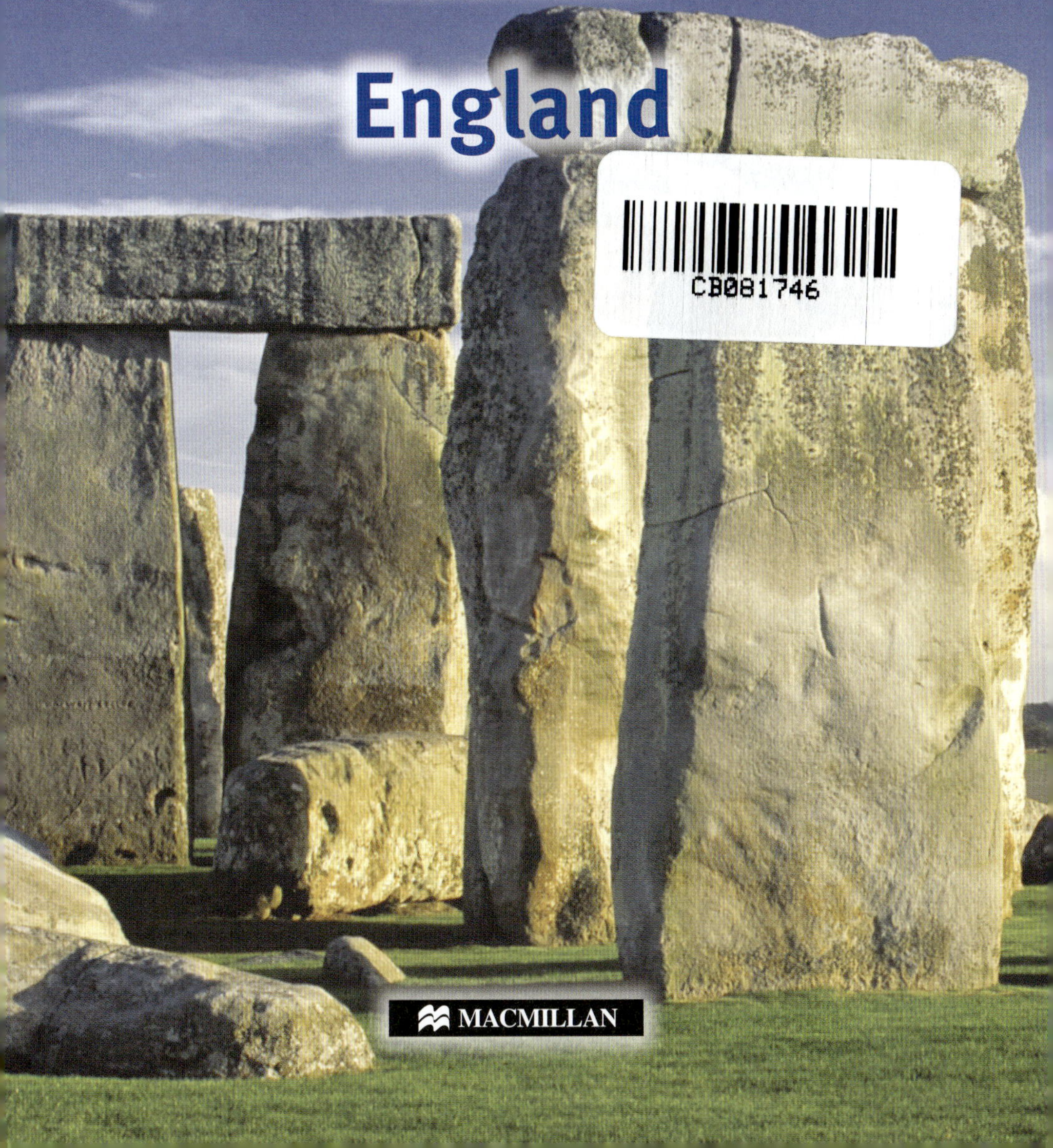



MACMILLAN

MACMILLAN CULTURAL READERS

**PRE-INTERMEDIATE LEVEL**

*Founding Editor of the Macmillan Readers:* John Milne

The Macmillan Readers provide a choice of enjoyable reading materials for learners of English. The series is published at six levels – Starter, Beginner, Elementary, Pre-intermediate, Intermediate and Upper. The Macmillan Cultural Readers are a factual strand of the series.

**Level Control**
Information, structure and vocabulary are controlled to suit the students' ability at each level.

**The number of words at each level:**

|  |  |
|---|---|
| Starter | about 300 basic words |
| Beginner | about 600 basic words |
| Elementary | about 1100 basic words |
| Pre-intermediate | about 1400 basic words |
| Intermediate | about 1600 basic words |
| Upper | about 2200 basic words |

**Vocabulary**
Some difficult words and phrases in this book are important for understanding the text. Some of these words are explained in the text, some are shown in the pictures and others are marked with a number like this: [3]. Phrases are marked with [P]. Words with a number are explained in the *Glossary* at the end of the book and phrases are explained on the *Useful Phrases* page.

**Answer Keys**
Answer Keys for the *Points For Understanding* and *Exercises* sections can be found at www.macmillanenglish.com/readers.

**Audio Download**
There is an audio download available to buy for this title. Visit www.macmillanenglish.com/readers for more information.

# Contents

# The Places In The Book

# Welcome To England

England is only a small country: about 640 kilometres from north to south, and 480 kilometres across its widest part. But some of the world's greatest writers are from England, and many of the most popular sports started there. In England, you can find busy, exciting cities, some of the oldest buildings in the world and also beautiful countryside. English society[1] today is modern with people from lots of different countries and cultures, but the country also has an amazing and long history. And, of course, its language is one of the most widely spoken in the world.

Between the Atlantic Ocean and the North Sea, England is part of the island of Great Britain, with Scotland to the north and Wales to the west. The country has forty-five counties – areas that often have their own council to lead them. England is not a big country, but some areas are very different from others. People in different parts of the country talk differently too!

England has a monarchy – it is ruled by a king or queen – but it also has an elected parliament[2], chosen by the people. The government is led[3] by the prime minister. Over fifty million people live in England. That is a lot of people for such a small country!

**Here are some important facts about England.**

**Population:** 52,234,000 (2010)

**Capital city:** London

**Biggest cities:** London, Liverpool, Birmingham, Manchester and Nottingham

**Highest mountain:** Scafell Pike, Lake District, 978 m

- People often incorrectly use the name England when they want to talk about Great Britain or the United Kingdom (UK).
- Great Britain is England, Scotland and Wales.
- The United Kingdom is England, Scotland, Wales and Northern Ireland. Its full name is The United Kingdom of Great Britain and Northern Ireland.
- The British Isles are England, Scotland, Wales, Ireland and over 6,000 smaller islands.

## Warm-up Quiz

How much do you know about England or think you know? Try these quiz questions and then read on to check your answers!

**1** Which of these sports started in England?
- **a** football
- **b** rugby
- **c** tennis

**2** Does England have …?
- **a** a queen
- **b** a king
- **c** a king and a queen

**3** Which of these animals might you see in England?
- **a** a fox
- **b** a bear
- **c** a deer

**4** What is the name of England's most famous music festival?
- **a** Glastonbury
- **b** Hay
- **c** Stonehenge

**5** Which of these writers are English?
- **a** Charles Dickens
- **b** William Shakespeare
- **c** JK Rowling

**6** Which of these things can you not do in England?
- **a** climb a mountain
- **b** travel on the *Titanic*
- **c** visit the home of The Beatles

**7** Which of these foods are not part of an English breakfast?
- **a** eggs
- **b** mushrooms
- **c** Yorkshire pudding

**8** Which is the biggest city in England?
- **a** Manchester
- **b** Birmingham
- **c** London

**9** Which university does not race in a famous boat race on the Thames?
- **a** Oxford
- **b** Cambridge
- **c** London

# 1 A Short History

**Hadrian's Wall, built by the Romans**

Back in England's oldest times, people lived in big groups called tribes. They were farmers – they grew their food, and kept animals for meat and eggs. They lived in villages, in wooden or mud[4] houses, and there was often fighting between the different tribes. Life was simple but dangerous.

Then in AD 43, forty thousand Roman soldiers invaded[5] England from the area of Europe that is now Italy. The Roman army was very well-organized and had good weapons[6]. The soldiers built a wall around themselves every night so they were safe. They moved across the country, fighting and winning battles[7] against the different tribes, and after four years they controlled[8] the south of England.

The Romans had to fight for many years before they controlled all of England. They made many changes in the country, such as building towns and cities, and good roads. They brought a new language to England – Latin – and made laws, so people knew what they could and could not do. The religion[9] of Christianity came to England in Roman times too.

The Romans never took control of[P] Scotland, which is north of England, and Scottish tribes came to fight against them in the north of England again and again. Because of this, in the second century AD, the Romans built a wall to stop the Scottish tribes coming to England. This wall between England and Scotland was one hundred and twenty kilometres long, and was called Hadrian's Wall.

For English people in towns and cities, life in Roman times was good. Towns now had clean water and sewers (pipes taking away dirty water), and there were strong walls around them, so people felt safe. People came to the towns to buy and sell things, and food became more interesting and enjoyable. To relax, people could go to special bath houses, where they met their friends, kept clean and exercised.

But after AD 250, Roman soldiers began to leave England. They had to fight in other parts of the world, and it was too expensive and difficult for them to keep England safe. By AD 411, all the Roman soldiers had left England. Then the Anglo-Saxons, from Germany, the Netherlands and Denmark, began to arrive. The Anglo-Saxons had come to England several times before, but the Romans had always defeated[12] them. Now, with the Romans gone, the English could not win battles against the Anglo-Saxons, and many Anglo-Saxons came to live in England.

The Anglo-Saxons did not like the Romans' towns, so they did not use them, and the towns stayed empty. The Anglo-Saxons built their own villages near rivers or the sea and made

> **i**
>
> There are many stories in England about King Arthur, who fought against the Anglo-Saxons. No one knows if King Arthur ever really lived, but he is important in a lot of English art, music and literature[10]. One famous story about Arthur is the story of the sword[11] in the stone. Arthur was the son of King Uther, but these were dangerous times in England, and Arthur's family wanted to keep him safe. So when Arthur was a baby, he was taken to live with another family, who took care of him along with their own son Kay. When King Uther died, no one knew that he had a son. The important people in England did not know who should be the next king. But then they saw a strange white stone with a sword in it. Gold writing on the stone said, 'The man who can pull out this sword will be King.' Many men tried to pull out the sword, but no one could move it. One day Arthur, who was looking for a sword for Kay, pulled it out. Then everyone knew he was the next king.

wooden houses. In their villages, they grew crops – plants they could use for food. They also kept pigs, sheep and cows, and caught fish and other animals.

> **i** In the AD 780s, the King of Mercia built a big ditch – a long, deep hole – between his kingdom and Wales. It was called Offa's Dyke, and you can see parts of it between Wales and England today.

By AD 600 in England, the Anglo-Saxons had made seven kingdoms – different parts of the country, each controlled by its own king. The four main kingdoms were Northumbria, Mercia, East Anglia and Wessex. The three minor kingdoms were Essex, Kent and Sussex. In each of these kingdoms, the king had nobles – important men who fought for him. The other people in the kingdom were either peasants or slaves. Peasants were poor people who had some land, but had to give money to the nobles. Slaves had nothing and had to work for other people for no money at all. People bought and sold slaves like animals.

The Anglo-Saxons stayed in England, but in AD 793 a new group of people invaded the country. The Vikings, from Norway, Sweden and Denmark, wanted good farming land. They came to England in strong wooden ships, and soon they took control of many parts of the country. But the Anglo-Saxon king of Wessex, Alfred the Great, won a big battle against the Vikings. After this, part of England, called Danelaw, was given to the Vikings, but the Vikings had to promise not to invade other parts of the country.

After Alfred the Great died, the Viking and Anglo-Saxon parts of England came together, and England was now ruled as one country with one king. The Vikings and the Anglo-Saxons continued to fight a lot, and for a while England had Viking kings, but by 1042, the Anglo-Saxon King Edward ruled England.

> **i** The names of many places in England tell us about their history. Towns with 'chester' or 'cester' on the end of the name, e.g. Manchester (/ˈmæntʃɪstə/) and Gloucester (/ˈglɒstə/), were Roman towns. The Anglo-Saxon for 'town' was 'burh', so towns like Scarborough (/ˈskɑːbərə/) and Peterborough (/ˈpiːtəˌbərə) were Anglo-Saxon. Towns with names ending in 'by', e.g. Derby (/ˈdɑːbi/) and Rugby (/ˈrʌgbi/), are Viking towns.

With Edward as the king, London became the most important city in England. Edward had many nobles,

and he let them become very powerful[13]. He had no children, so when he died, one of his nobles, Harold, became the king. But Edward's cousin William, a Norman (from the north of France), believed that he should be the king of England. In October 1066, William brought a big Norman army from France to England. The Normans fought against Harold and his soldiers at the Battle of Hastings. Harold was killed, and William the Conqueror[14], as he was called, became the king of England.

The French made a beautiful tapestry showing the story of William's invasion of England and the Battle of Hastings. You can see this today in Normandy.

**The Bayeux Tapestry**

William the Conqueror made many important changes in England. A lot of castles were built. One of these was the Tower of London, which you can visit today. William the Conqueror brought the feudal system to England. In the feudal system, the richest and most important person was the king. Below the king were the nobles, then the knights and then the serfs, who were the poorest people in the land. The king owned everything in the country, but he gave a castle and land to his nobles, and they paid him money. The nobles gave land to the knights, who had to fight battles for the nobles and the king. The knights gave some land to the serfs, who had to work for the knights and give them food from the land.

William the Conqueror wanted to know exactly what he had in England. He sent people all around the country, asking many questions, and they made a big book called the Domesday Book. The book showed how much farming land there was in England and how many animals. We know a lot about life in Norman England because of the Domesday Book.

The time from William the Conqueror's rule until the fifteenth century in England is often called the Middle Ages. In the Middle Ages, most people lived in villages. The people of the village had to work for the nobles, and give them crops and animals. The nobles lived very well, in big houses and with expensive food, but most people were very poor.

Religion was very important in the Middle Ages, and the Catholic Church became very powerful. From 1095 to 1291, soldiers went to other countries to fight religious battles. There was more fighting in the fourteenth and fifteenth centuries, as France and England fought the Hundred Years War, hoping to win land from each other. Many of the battles of the Hundred Years War were fought by knights. As well as fighting battles for nobles and for the king, knights also fought as a sport in competitions[15] called jousting tournaments. Young men who wanted to become knights had to spend many years learning all the things that a knight could do.

**Armoured knights jousting at a tournament in the Middle Ages**

In 1348, a terrible illness called The Black Death came to England. Only about four million people lived in England at that time, but in two years, nearly one-and-a-half million of them died.

From 1455–1485, there were terrible battles between people who wanted the kings of the country to be from different families, and many more people died. Finally, in 1485, Henry Tudor became the first Tudor king of England, King Henry the Seventh.

Some of the Tudor kings and queens are now very famous in England's history. Henry the Eighth, who became the king in 1509, lived some of the time at the Tower of London, but he had other beautiful palaces in and around London, including the Palace of Westminster and Hampton Court. He and the people around him lived very well. They wore the best clothes and ate wonderful food, and at the palaces there was always dancing, sport, poetry and music. Henry enjoyed life, and he drank and ate too much. When he became the king, he was a sporty, good-looking young man, but later he became so fat he could not walk!

England was a Catholic country, but Henry the Eighth wanted England to leave the Catholic Church, so he started a new church. It was a Protestant church (a Christian church, but for people who believe in a different kind of Christianity) called the Church of England, and he controlled it. Anyone who disagreed with the new church was executed – killed for their crime. When Henry the Eighth was ruling England, more than seventy thousand people were killed because of crimes, or because they disagreed with the king about religion or other important things.

> Henry the Eighth had six wives! He ended his marriage with two of them, and executed another two. One died, and one was alive when he died in 1547.

Six years after Henry the Eighth died, his oldest daughter Mary – the daughter he had with his first wife, Catherine of Aragon – became Queen Mary the First of England. She was a Catholic and wanted England to be a Catholic country again, but many people had left the Catholic Church and had become Protestants. Mary executed hundreds of Protestants who refused to become Catholic again.

But in 1558, Mary died, and her half-sister Elizabeth – the daughter Henry had with his second wife Anne Boleyn – became the queen. Queen Elizabeth the First was a Protestant, but she did not make Catholics follow her religion, and she soon became one of the best loved of England's kings and queens.

The second half of the sixteenth century, which was known as the Elizabethan period, was a very important time for English literature. Many people liked to go to the theatre, and William Shakespeare wrote a lot of plays and poetry at this time. Ships also began to travel to other parts of the world. Sir Walter Raleigh sailed to America, and Sir Francis Drake became the first Englishman to sail around the world.

But life in England was also very difficult for many people in the Elizabethan period. There was less work in farming now, and a lot of people were very poor. There was a lot of crime, but no police, and when people were caught for crimes, they were often executed.

After Queen Elizabeth the First died in 1603, kings and queens called the Stuarts came to power[16] in England. The Stuarts were from Scotland, and for the first time, they ruled both England and Scotland. The second of the Stuart kings was Charles the First. He argued with Parliament because he spent a lot of money fighting wars in Europe, and in 1642, he started a civil war[17]. For seven years, the King's men and Parliament's men fought against each other, and thousands died. But with Oliver Cromwell as leader, Parliament's army became very strong and fought very well, and in 1649, they won the war. Charles the First was executed, and for eleven years England had no king or queen. The country was ruled by Cromwell and Parliament. Cromwell was a Puritan – a Protestant who believed in a simple, hard-working life – and when he ruled, there was no sport or dancing in England, and theatres were closed.

When Cromwell died, England was ready to have a king again, and the Stuarts came to power once more. There were some difficult times for England in the second half of the seventeenth century. In 1665, another terrible illness came to London and killed nearly seventy thousand people, and a year later, large parts of London were burnt down in the Great Fire of London.

There were many other changes at this time too. England now traded – bought and sold things – with many other countries, so English people could get different foods like tomatoes, chocolate, coffee and tea for the first time. People continued to work on the land, but now there were other jobs, in cloth[18]-making or glass-making, and in the coal[19] or iron[20] industries[21]. London was rebuilt with wider roads and many beautiful new buildings, and scientists like Sir Isaac Newton began to do important work and learn many interesting things. England started its first colonies too. These were other parts of the world, like America, which were ruled by England. For the first time in the seventeenth century, people from England went to live and work in these places.

There was one more important change as England entered the eighteenth century. In 1707, the Act of Union brought England, Wales and Scotland together with one parliament as Great Britain.

The eighteenth and early nineteenth centuries were called the Georgian period because Britain's kings were George the First, Second, Third and Fourth. But during this time, kings became much less powerful, and Parliament really began to rule the country. An industrial revolution began in Britain too: machines were built, and they were used in many different industries. People could now make many things very quickly, and because of this towns began to grow.

> In 1814, George Stephenson made the first steam engine[22] for trains, and in 1830, one of the first railways, between Liverpool and Manchester, was opened. Now people and things could move from one place to another much more quickly than ever before.

In 1783, Britain lost the American War of Independence, so America was no longer ruled by Britain and became independent[23]. Britain did not have its old American colonies anymore, but it now found new ones. In that same year, France gave its colonies in Canada to Britain, and by the end of the eighteenth century, Britain had won many battles in India, which soon became an important part of the British Empire[24]. This was a great time for exploration: travelling to different places to find new things. The famous sailor Captain Cook visited many new lands and was the first European to go to Australia and New Zealand.

In 1801, Ireland and Britain came together as the United Kingdom (UK) with one parliament. (Today, Northern Ireland is the only part of Ireland which belongs to the UK.) The ruler of this new UK, from 1837 until 1901, was Queen Victoria. Victoria ruled for longer than any other English or British king or queen, and she was much loved by many of her people. In the Victorian period, the British

> In the Victorian period, very poor people with no homes went to live in places called workhouses. Here they were given very little food and had to work very hard. Charles Dickens wrote about the workhouses in his famous book *Oliver Twist*.

Empire became bigger and more important, and the industrial revolution continued. The country was growing, but at first this made life difficult for many people. More and more factories[25] were built in the UK, and factory work was very hard and very dangerous. Towns got bigger and bigger, but people put their rubbish[26] and dirty water in the streets, so there was a lot of illness.

***The Wealth of England: The Bessemer Process of Making Steel*, William Holt Yates Titcomb, 1895**

But soon important new changes started to happen. Towns became cleaner, and in 1880, all children aged 5–10 began to go to school. People had electric lights and telephones for the first time, and because the railways grew, they could now travel around the country easily. By 1901, when Queen Victoria died, the modern United Kingdom was arriving.

| AD 43 | AD 450 | AD 793 | 1066 | 1485 | 1603 | 1714 | 1837 | 1901 |
|---|---|---|---|---|---|---|---|---|
| Romans | Anglo-Saxons | Vikings | Middle Ages | Tudors | Stuarts | Georgians | Victorians | Modern United Kingdom |

# 2 England in the Modern UK

*A nation which has forgotten its past can have no future.*

**Winston Churchill, prime minister 1940–45, 1951–55**

**Modern London**

In the early 1900s, the UK was one of the most powerful countries in the world, with a big empire. The industrial revolution was changing many people's lives, and steamships and cars were widely used for the first time.

Rich people lived very well, with beautiful houses and servants, but poor people had few clothes and little to eat, and their children were often ill. Life was difficult for women in the UK at this time too. People expected women to stay at home with their families, and they could not get well-paid jobs. It was very difficult for women to go to university, and they could not vote[28]. In 1903, a group of women called the suffragettes, led by Emmeline Pankhurst, organized meetings and marches[29], asking for Parliament to give women the vote.

> In April 1912, a new steamship called the *Titanic* sailed from England for New York City. The *Titanic* was the biggest and fastest ship in the world. It was also very comfortable, with libraries, restaurants and a swimming pool. But after only a few days at sea, it hit ice and sank[27], killing 1,517 people.

Some suffragettes went to prison for their beliefs, and one, Emily Davison, ran in front of the King's horse at a horse race[30] in 1913. She died a few days later.

**English suffragettes**

In 1914, the UK and its allies[31], France and Russia, went to war with Germany and Austria-Hungary. Many young men chose to fight. They believed the war would be very short, but it went on for four years, and nearly three quarters of a million soldiers from the UK were killed. While the men were fighting, women had to do the men's jobs at home. Women soon showed that they could work in farming, factories and even in the coal industry.

After helping their country to win the First World War, workers and women in England wanted better lives. Men got their jobs at home back from the women, so most women were no longer working, but in 1918, women over thirty were given the vote for the first time. From 1929, women, like men, could vote from the age of twenty-one. A new political[32] party for working people – the Labour Party – became important in politics at this time, and in 1926, half a million workers went on strike[P] to fight against low pay and long working hours. But life became even more difficult for workers in 1929, when the world went into an economic depression[33]. Prices[34] fell, there was less trade, and many shops and factories closed. By 1931, nearly three million people in the UK had lost their jobs.

The First World War was fought mainly in battles on fields in France, but almost everyone in the UK had a difficult life because of the Second World War (1939–45). Many children had to leave their homes and go to live in the countryside. This was because at the end of 1940 and the beginning of 1941, the Germans dropped many bombs[35] on London and other cities. This was called the Blitz. Many people lost their homes and their families, and everyone had to live on rations – they could only buy fixed amounts of many kinds of food.

**London during the Blitz**

'When we heard the air raid warning in the middle of the night, everyone woke up and got into the shelters.

'On the first night of the Blitz, we stayed in there with my mother and our relatives. My mother said all the noises were guns, but we really knew they were bombs. We were so frightened. I was crying because I was terrified of the noise.'

**ALF MORRIS, LONDON**

The Second World War ended in 1945, and big changes were made by a new Labour government. Most importantly, the UK now had a National Health Service, so anyone who was ill could see a doctor or go to hospital without paying. The government also now gave money to help people who were ill or old, or had lost their jobs. Because of the Education[36] Act of 1944, there were also free places in schools for children up to the age of fifteen.

Another change after the Second World War was that more women went to work. They had shown that they could do men's jobs, and many of them had done important war work. In some homes, nothing was different for women, but over the next fifty years, women in the UK slowly saw changes for themselves in education, work and at home. Their lives would never be the same again.

After the Second World War, many of the UK's colonies wanted to rule themselves. The south of Ireland had already become independent from the UK in 1921, so the country had now become the United Kingdom of Great Britain and Northern Ireland. People from the colonies had fought for the UK during the war, and they felt they had won their freedom. In 1947, India, once a very important part of the Empire, became independent. In the next twenty years, most of the other colonies also did the same. They became independent, but joined the Commonwealth, an organization of the governments of the UK's old colonies.

The UK needed more workers to help rebuild the country after the war, so the government invited other Europeans and people from the colonies of the old Empire to move there. Hoping to find good new jobs, many people came, mainly from Europe, India, Pakistan and the West Indies. In 1945, there were only a few thousand non-white people in the UK, but by 1970, there were 1.4 million. Sadly, there were often problems in later years when some of the people born in the UK felt that immigrants[37] and their families were taking too many jobs. There is some racism – when people do not like others because they have a different colour skin – in the UK today. But most people do not like racism and want all people in the UK to live together happily.

In 1952, Elizabeth the Second became the new queen of the UK, and millions of people watched her coronation[38] on TV. The first TVs were made in the 1920s, but many English people bought TVs for the first time for the coronation, and in the 1950s, TV started to become an important part of life in England.

There were many changes in the UK in the second half of the twentieth century. Many of the country's traditional industries, for example iron, cloth, coal and shipbuilding, began to have problems, and people working in those industries lost their jobs. New industries became more important, for example banking and pharmaceuticals (drugs and medicines).

> In August every year, there is a big street festival in London called the Notting Hill Carnival. The Notting Hill Carnival first began in 1965, to celebrate the music, dance and traditions of the many Caribbean people living in London. Today, it is the second biggest street festival in the world.

England today is a very different place than it was one hundred years ago. Today, England is one of the most multicultural[39] countries in the world, and many people from the West Indies, Africa, India, China, South-East Asia and eastern Europe live here. More than two hundred and fifty different languages are spoken in London! Probably because of this, there are also many religions in England. England is a Christian country, but different religions are freely followed, and there are many Hindu, Jewish, Muslim, Sikh and Buddhist people here.

**Multicultural England today**

Society has changed in England too. One hundred years ago, most people married in their early twenties or younger and then had children, but today many more people live alone, and most do not get married or have children until they are in their thirties or older.

**The wedding of Prince William and Catherine Middleton**

England's place in the world, as part of the UK, is also very different. The UK does not have an empire now, but it is an important country in Europe and became a member of the European Union (then called the EEC) in 1973. The UK works very closely with the United States of America (USA), and it also continues to be a member of the Commonwealth, together with fifty-two other countries from around the world. Members of the Commonwealth meet every two years to decide how they can best work together.

> In 1994, the Channel Tunnel was built, taking a railway under the sea between England and France.

# 3 Traditions

> *The people of England are the most enthusiastic[40] in the world.*
>
> **Benjamin Disraeli, Prime Minister**

**Morris dancing in London**

Because England is such an old country, it has many traditions. Some of these have come from important or interesting moments in history. Some have come from other parts of the world. Others have come from England's many kings or queens, or from its long religious history.

There are special days and festivals throughout the year in England, but only a few are bank holidays – days when people do not have to work. Christmas is one of the most important religious festivals in England. Christmas Day, 25th December, and the next day, Boxing Day, are always bank holidays, and most people spend this time with family or friends. Traditionally, people eat turkey[41] on Christmas Day, with Brussels sprouts and cranberry sauce; and for dessert there is usually Christmas pudding, a type of cake made with dried fruit.

Not long before Christmas, people decorate[42] their houses and send cards to people they know. On Christmas Day, there are presents from friends and family, and, for the children, from Father Christmas (or Santa Claus). Children believe that Father Christmas brings the presents on 24$^{th}$ December, Christmas Eve, and leaves them to be opened on the morning of Christmas Day.

> i
>
> People in England first began to have Christmas trees after Queen Victoria's husband Prince Albert brought one from Germany to Windsor Castle in 1841.
>
> Every year a big Christmas tree is sent from Norway and put in Trafalgar Square, Central London. The tree is a present from the people of Norway to thank the UK for its help in the Second World War.

**An English Christmas dinner: turkey, Brussels sprouts and cranberry sauce**

New Year's Eve is also important in England. Many people go to the Houses of Parliament in London to hear Big Ben (the bell inside the big clock tower) strike[43] midnight and to see the wonderful fireworks[44] near the River Thames. Other people meet up with friends and family, and make New Year's Resolutions: they decide what things they will do (or not do!) in the next year.

On Valentine's Day, 14$^{th}$ February, people give cards or presents to the people they love, but April Fool's Day, on 1$^{st}$ April, is a very different kind of celebration[45]. On that day, people play jokes on their friends and family, and call them an 'April Fool!'. People think April Fool's Day started because, before 1562, 1$^{st}$ April was the first day of the year. In 1562, this was changed, so 1$^{st}$ January became the first day of the year. But many people were slow to remember the change, so they were laughed at for celebrating New Year's Day on 1$^{st}$ April.

'I remember one year I was watching the television with my parents, and there were pictures of spaghetti[46] trees. Women were picking the spaghetti from the trees and then putting it in the sun to dry.

'"But spaghetti doesn't grow on trees, does it?" my father said. My mother went and looked in the dictionary. We all knew that spaghetti doesn't grow on trees, but there it was on the television! Then suddenly we remembered – it was April Fool's Day!'

**JENNETTA KIDDLE, LEICESTER**

There is often special food for festivals in England. Shrove Tuesday, in February, comes the day before the start of Lent, the forty days before Easter. In the past, people stopped eating the most important foods – butter, eggs and flour – during Lent. So on Shrove Tuesday, they made pancakes[47] with these foods, and ate butter, eggs and flour for the last time. People continue to eat pancakes today, and there are many pancake races around the country: people have to run, throwing pancakes up and down in a frying pan[48]! Today, many people try to give something up[P] for Lent too – often sweets, cakes or chocolate!

### Recipe for pancakes

Put 110 g flour in a bowl with a little bit of salt. Break two eggs into the bowl and whisk[49] them into the flour. Then put in 200 ml milk and 75 ml water, whisking all the time. Melt[50] some butter in a frying pan and put in some of the mixture, covering the bottom of the pan. Cook for about ten seconds, then turn the pancake and cook the other side. Eat it with sugar and lemon juice, bananas or chocolate!

**Pancakes**

After Lent comes Easter, another religious festival, and for people who go to church, a very important time of year. Easter comes in the spring, and many people give each other Easter eggs and Easter bunnies (little rabbits) made from chocolate. For children, there are often Easter Egg Hunts, when little eggs are hidden in the house or garden. People also eat hot cross buns at Easter – warm sweet bread with dried fruit inside and a cross on top.

May Day in England is on the first day of May, and there is a bank holiday on or very near that day. This is usually the start of warmer weather in England, and sometimes people celebrate with Maypole dancing – dancing around a big pole[51] with ribbons[52].

Halloween, on 31st October, has become a popular festival in modern times. On this night, children dress up as witches, ghosts and other frightening things, and go from house to house, calling 'Trick or Treat'. The neighbours give them sweets and other nice things, but if they have nothing to give, the children play a trick, or joke, on them.

A strange festival is held on 5th November. On that day in 1605, a man called Guy Fawkes and a group of friends tried to blow up[53] the Houses of Parliament. They wanted to do this because King James and his nobles were not treating[54] the Catholics in the country well. But the king's soldiers found Guy Fawkes in the Houses of Parliament and stopped him and his friends.

Now on 5th November every year, there are bonfires[55] and fireworks all over England on 'Guy Fawkes Night'.

Another day that is important because of something in history is Remembrance Day, on 11th November. At eleven o'clock in the morning on that day, at exactly the time when the First World War ended in 1918, many people are silent for two minutes. They remember the many men and women who have lost their lives in wars. Many people wear paper poppies – red flowers – on their coats at this time too. Poppies grew on the battlefields of France after the First World War ended, so they make people remember the terrible days of the war.

Because kings and queens have always been so important in England's history, there are many royal[56] traditions. One important tradition is the State Opening of Parliament. On this day, the Queen goes from her home at Buckingham Palace to the Houses of Parliament in a gold carriage[57] and then reads 'the Queen's speech[58]'. This tells people what the government wants to do in the next year.

Another important yearly royal tradition is called 'Trooping the Colour'. To celebrate the Queen's birthday, more than a thousand soldiers and musicians march from Buckingham Palace to Whitehall and back again, and the Queen goes past them in her carriage.

**Trooping the Colour**

On most days at Buckingham Palace, you can also see the 'Changing of the Guard'. This is when one group of soldiers who were guarding[59] the Queen leave the palace, and another group arrives. The soldiers who guard the Queen wear red coats and tall hats, made from real bearskin[60]. They can march in front of the palace, but when they are standing, they must not move.

There are many important traditions in sport in England. One famous example is the Oxford and Cambridge boat race. Oxford and Cambridge are the two oldest universities in England, and because both universities are in cities with rivers, Oxford and Cambridge students have always enjoyed rowing. In rowing, two, four or eight people move a boat through water with long wooden sticks called oars. They sit with their backs towards the front of the boat, so there is often a person called a cox at the back, telling them where to go. In 1829, students from Oxford and Cambridge decided to have a rowing race, and since then there has been a race on the Thames every year in spring.

**The Oxford and Cambridge boat race: Oxford in dark blue, Cambridge in light blue**

What is traditional English food and drink? Fish and chips are probably England's most famous dish. Fish and chips first became popular in the 1860s, when the railways opened and trains began to bring fish from the east coast of England to the cities. Fish and chips are usually eaten as take-away food (food that is not eaten in a café or restaurant), with the fish wrapped in paper, and the chips covered in salt and vinegar[61]. Today, Indian and Chinese take-aways are just as popular as fish and chips.

England is also famous for its breakfasts. Very few people eat a full English breakfast every day, but you can usually get one in hotels or cafés. The English breakfast is toast, eggs and sausages[62], often with tomatoes, beans, hashbrowns (potato cakes) and mushrooms too!

**A traditional English breakfast**

Bangers (sausages) and mash (a mixture of potatoes with butter and milk) is another traditional dish in England. The sausages are often called bangers because in times of war, when food was rationed, there was usually a lot of water in the sausages. When they were fried, they often blew up!

The traditional Sunday lunch is a roast dinner, with roast beef, roast potatoes and Yorkshire pudding (a cooked mixture of eggs, flour and milk). However, many English people now eat fewer traditional dishes, and English people now eat lots of different kinds of food from all around the world. But some traditional English food continues to be very popular. English farmers make wonderful cheeses like red leicester, cheddar and stilton, and at farmers' markets all around the country people can buy fantastic meat, fish, fruit, vegetables and bread.

Tea, of course, is one of the most important drinks in England, and in cafés and at home many people like to have afternoon tea, which is tea with cakes and sandwiches.

> *The Englishman who visits Mount Etna will carry[63] his tea-kettle to the top.*
>
> **Ralph Waldo Emerson, American poet**

English people also like to go to the pub to have a drink and perhaps to eat. These are places where people come together to talk, play games, or watch football or rugby matches.

> In England, people drink 100 million cups of tea every day! That's a lot of tea!

### How to make a perfect cup of tea

First warm the teapot – put some boiling water in the teapot for a few seconds and then empty the teapot. Then put one spoonful of tea for each person into the teapot, with one extra spoonful. Put boiling water in and leave it for a few minutes.

**spoonful** = an amount of food the same size as a spoon
**teapot** = a pot used for making tea
**boiling** = very, very hot

In different areas of England there are some very strange traditions. At many fairs[64], you can see morris dancing (people in costumes[65] dancing to music with sticks, swords and handkerchiefs). In the Lake District, people have a 'gurning' competition every year. Gurning is trying to make a very strange face, for example by lifting the bottom of your mouth up above the top of it! And in a village near Gloucester there is a cheese-rolling competition, in which people run after a cheese which is moving like a wheel down a very big hill!

i

There are many traditional sayings in England. What do you think these ones mean? Match the saying with its meaning.

1 Make hay while the sun shines.
2 Out of the frying pan, into the fire.
3 The grass is always greener on the other side.

a We always think other people's lives are better than ours.
b Do things when you can.
c From one bad thing to another thing that is even worse.

# 4 Cities and Sights

*When a man is tired of London, he is tired of life; for there is in London all that life can afford.*

**Samuel Johnson**

**all that life can afford** = everything that life can give

**London – England's capital city**

England has fifty cities and many smaller towns, and there are lots of things to see and do there.

The biggest city, and England's capital, is London. Nearly eight million people live in London – more than in any other European city. The country's government is there, and for people in many different jobs, London is the most important place to be for work.

For visitors, too, London has many of England's most interesting sights and is one of the most important places to visit. London has many areas, which are often very different, even if they are very close!

Whitehall and Westminster are the areas where you can see some of London's most famous sights. Here, next to the River Thames, are Big Ben

'London is massive – really, really big. You can go where you want on the underground, the train that travels under the ground. You can travel miles in only a few minutes – but it's still too big. Even meeting a friend takes so much time – he tells you to go to this stop, turn right, turn left, but it's impossible to find him.'

**XAVI CALAFELL, SPAIN**

and the Houses of Parliament. At one time, England's kings and queens lived in these buildings, and they were called the Palace of Westminster, but today Parliament meets here. Near the Houses of Parliament is Downing Street, where the UK's prime minister – the leader – lives, and where the government meets. Also near here is Westminster Abbey, a large and very important church where England's kings and queens have had their coronations since the time of William the Conqueror.

Following the Thames to the north, and then towards the east from Whitehall and Westminster, you come to the West End. Here you can find theatres, restaurants, cinemas and clubs. Covent Garden, where there was once a big market, is now a great place to go shopping, or to have a coffee and watch the street entertainers – actors, musicians, dancers and others who do small shows outside.

Further east is a small area called the City of London, which was the most important part of London in the Middle Ages. It is now one of the great financial centres of the world – a place where money comes in and out, and where England's big banks work from. Also here is St Paul's Cathedral, which was built by the great architect[66] Sir Christopher Wren, and the Tower of London, a castle from the eleventh century.

London is also famous for its large and beautiful parks. Just minutes from the West End, people can walk,

For more than eight hundred years, from 1101, people were kept in prison at the Tower of London and also executed. The last execution at the Tower of London was in 1941, during the Second World War.

exercise and relax in the large green areas of Hyde Park, Green Park and St James's Park. Many people visit London for its museums[67] and art galleries, and most of these are free. The Tate Modern is the world's largest modern art gallery, and at the British Museum, there are several kilometres of rooms, with more than seventy thousand things to see.

Many visitors to London like to take a ride on the London Eye, the largest Ferris wheel[68] in Europe. From the top of the Eye, at one hundred and thirty-five metres, you can see many of London's most famous buildings.

Not far from London, you can visit three interesting and important royal places – Windsor Castle, which continues to be used by the royal family today, Hampton Court Palace and Kew Gardens.

It is less than 100 kilometres from London to Oxford, one of England's most beautiful cities and home to its oldest university. Here you can walk around the fantastic old buildings of colleges like Christ Church and Magdalen, many of them more than five hundred years old. Oxford also has England's oldest museum, the Ashmolean, as well as parks, gardens and lovely river walks.

Oxford is near a famous area of England called the Cotswolds. Close to the green hills there are beautiful villages, with pretty houses made from gold-coloured stone and fine old churches. Many visitors come to this area, and there are tourist shops and afternoon tea rooms in a lot of the bigger villages.

> There are about eleven million books in Oxford's famous Bodleian libraries, and many of them are kept in big rooms under the ground below the libraries.

Oxford is not very far from Stratford-upon-Avon, famous as the home town of William Shakespeare, the great writer. In this pretty river town, you can visit Shakespeare's old house and also see a play at the theatre of the Royal Shakespeare Company.

At Warwick, just a few kilometres away, is one of the greatest medieval castles in England. With its great towers and walls, dark dungeons[69] and beautiful gardens, Warwick Castle is one of the most impressive in England.

The University of Cambridge is almost as old as Oxford's, and the two cities are like each other in many ways. Like Oxford, Cambridge is a city of old colleges, many from the late thirteenth and early fourteenth centuries. With its gardens, green spaces and river, Cambridge is a lovely city to walk around. Two of the most famous places in Cambridge are King's College,

**The city of Oxford**

with its beautiful chapel (a small church), and the Backs, an area of green land around the River Cam from where you can see many of the colleges.

Moving north, England's second biggest city is Birmingham, which was an important centre during the industrial revolution. Today, Birmingham is a very multicultural city and is home to the National Exhibition Centre (NEC), where many big shows and events[70] are held. Many people come to Birmingham to visit its big, modern shopping centre, the Bull Ring, but few tourists spend a lot of time here.

Further north of Birmingham, Stoke-on-Trent has been famous since the seventeenth century for its pottery industry – the industry of making objects such as cups, plates and bowls. Here you can visit the pottery factories and buy pottery cheaply from the factory shops.

York is one of the most interesting cities of the north of England. It was a Roman city, and for many years it was an important place for religion and politics in England. During medieval times – the Middle Ages – there was a strong wool trade in York, and because of this, many other traders came to live here. The city feels very medieval even today, with its narrow streets and old walls. Many tourists come to visit the city and to see York Minster, the city's old cathedral (a large and important church), with its beautiful windows. York was an important city when the railways were first built in England, and now it is home to the National Railway Museum.

Twenty-five kilometres from York is Castle Howard, one of the best of England's stately homes (big country houses). Stately homes were built for the most important families of England, who normally had homes in London too. These homes were places where the king or queen could visit and where important people could have meetings about politics or government.

Two very exciting cities in the north of England are Liverpool and Manchester. Liverpool, which is on the sea, became important in the eighteenth century because of trade with America. Many immigrants from the West Indies, China and Ireland arrived in Liverpool when they came to England, so Liverpool was one of England's first multicultural cities. But by the 1970s and 1980s, ships were no longer coming to Liverpool. The city's old buildings stayed empty, and it became very poor. Since 2004, a lot of money has been spent in Liverpool, and Albert Dock, where ships used to arrive, is now an exciting new area with restaurants, museums, shops and art galleries.

Liverpool was home to The Beatles, and many people come here to do 'Beatles Tours' and to visit the clubs where the famous band[71] played or see the homes where John, Paul, George and Ringo lived. In Liverpool, you can also see some wonderful art at the Walker Art Gallery or Tate

> **i** Just outside Liverpool, on Crosby Beach, there are one hundred statues of men made from iron, looking out to sea. The group of statues is called *Another Place*, and it was made by the artist Antony Gormley. The statues were only expected to stay in Liverpool for a short time, but people liked them so much that they wanted them to stay there. The artist agreed, and the statues have now been on Crosby Beach since 2005.

**Liverpool, home of The Beatles**

Liverpool, visit the two cathedrals, or take a boat across the River Mersey and look back at the famous sights of this great city.

Just fifty kilometres east of Liverpool is another big city, Manchester. Manchester has some of the most exciting modern buildings in England. Its cafés, clubs and nightlife make it one of the best cities in the country for many young people. But like Liverpool, Manchester had a difficult time in the second half of the twentieth century. Once the most important city in the world for cotton, Manchester's old industries were coming to an end by the 1950s, and many people lost their jobs. But new industries began to grow, and at the start of the twenty-first century, parts of the city were rebuilt, making Manchester an exciting city once more.

Blackpool is very different from Liverpool and Manchester. With its long beaches, hotels and piers[72], Blackpool is a popular holiday town. Here you can eat fish and chips, go to amusement arcades[73] and see the coloured lights on Blackpool Tower.

Some of the most interesting sights of England are in the far north of the country. Durham Cathedral, almost nine hundred years old, is here, and also the *Angel of the North*, the biggest sculpture[74] in England. The sculpture – of an angel[75] with very wide wings – was built on an old coal mine[76] by Antony Gormley, the same artist who made *Another Place* (see the fact box opposite). He wanted people to remember that for two hundred years, mining was one of the biggest industries in this area.

People pass the *Angel of the North* as they drive to Newcastle upon Tyne. Like Manchester and Liverpool, Newcastle is another industrial city that now has museums, art galleries and an exciting nightlife.

Near Newcastle is the end of Hadrian's Wall, parts of which can be seen very clearly. Today, the border[77] with Scotland is further north than it was when the Romans built Hadrian's Wall. Just a few kilometres from today's border is another interesting sight, Holy Island, or Lindisfarne. You cannot get to the island at high tide – when the sea comes in closest to the land – but at other times you can walk or drive across to it and see the castle that was built here in the sixteenth century.

Back in the south of England, and west of London, there are more sights and interesting cities to see. Bath, so-called because of its famous Roman baths, is a lovely little city. The old Roman baths are some of the best-kept in Europe, and in the eighteenth century, many rich and important people came here to 'take the waters'. Big, fine houses were built for them, and so Bath has many Georgian streets and buildings, with pretty parks too.

Just a few kilometres further west from Bath, but very different, is the big, busy city of Bristol. Bristol, once a very big port[78], now has a strong electronics[79] industry and is important in the creative media – film, TV, radio and fashion. It is also the biggest cultural centre in the area, with a busy nightlife. As in many other cities in England, the old docks – the area where the ships used to come in – have now been changed into an area for restaurants, shops and museums. One of the most famous sights of Bristol is the Clifton Suspension Bridge, which was made by the great engineer[80] Isambard Kingdom Brunel.

Many visitors to Bristol make the short journey south to Glastonbury. Here you can visit Glastonbury Abbey, which was built in the seventh century. Glastonbury is also

'I think Bath is Britain's most beautiful little city. I love the fact that you can stand in any street in the city centre, look up and see the tops of green hills. On a sunny summer's day, there's nowhere more beautiful.'

**SAMANTHA LAW**

famous for the music festival held there most years in June. It is the biggest music festival in the country.

Stonehenge, east of Glastonbury, is one of the wonders of the world. The big stone circles here were made between 3000 BC and 1600 BC – they are as old as Egypt's pyramids[81]! One of the most interesting things about Stonehenge is that some of the stones are very heavy – up to forty tonnes – but they came from hundreds of kilometres away, in Wales. People believe they were probably brought and pulled to Stonehenge in simple boats. But no one is sure how they got to Stonehenge. On the longest day of the year, the sun rises across the stone circles. Because of this, many people think the circles were perhaps some kind of ancient[82] calendar.

**Stonehenge**

In the county of Cornwall, in the far south-west of England, you can visit the Eden Project. Here you can see plants and trees from many different places, and the largest non-wild rainforest[83] in the world.

Brighton, on the south coast, became an important town in the mid-eighteenth century, when people began to enjoy swimming in the sea. The Prince of Wales (later King George the Fourth) started to come to Brighton in the 1780s, and in 1815, the Royal Pavilion was built for him. The Royal Pavilion, which has a strange mixture of Indian and Chinese building styles, is one of the most interesting buildings in Brighton today. Like Bath, Brighton has some beautiful Georgian buildings, but it is a fun town too. Here you can walk on the pier, beside the sea, or through the Lanes – narrow streets that were once part of the old fishing village of Brighton, and which are now busy with shops and restaurants.

North-east of Brighton, on the road to Dover, Canterbury is a place full of history. It was an important Roman town, and in AD 602, the first cathedral in England was built here. The cathedral was rebuilt in 1070 and continues to be very important today: the Archbishop of Canterbury is the head of the Church of England.

As you can see, there are lots of exciting places to visit in England!

i

In 1162, Thomas à Becket became Archbishop of Canterbury, but he argued with the King, and in 1170, four knights killed him while he was in the cathedral. After this, people said that miracles – strange and wonderful things – began to happen in the cathedral. So people began to make pilgrimages – religious journeys – to visit Canterbury Cathedral. Between 1387 and 1400, Geoffrey Chaucer wrote about a group of pilgrims who travelled to Canterbury together, telling stories. *The Canterbury Tales* tell us a lot about England in the Middle Ages, and they continue to be very famous today.

# 5 Nature and the Environment

The Lake District, England's biggest national park

*'Oh, to be in England, now that April's there.'*

**Robert Browning, poet**

England has some exciting and beautiful cities, and many interesting sights. But for a lot of people, the best thing about England is its countryside. Mostly, England is a place of green hills, but it also has lakes, rivers, a long coastline that is very different in different parts of the country and, in the north, mountains. Because there are so many different kinds of environments in England, there is a lot of wildlife[84] too. Around the coast you can see seals, sharks, dolphins and otters; and rabbits, foxes, squirrels and deer are just some of the animals that move around the countryside freely. Nearly two hundred and thirty different kinds of birds live in England, and another two hundred visit for part of the year. There are also many different kinds of trees, plants and wild flowers growing in the English countryside.

The weather in England is temperate – almost never very, very hot, or very, very cold – with lots of rain all year. It is usually warmest between June and September, but the weather in any month can be very different from year to year.

rabbit

squirrel

badger

bat

red deer

butterfly

seal

golden
eagle

basking shark

porpoise

puffin

otter

robin

hedgehog

pony

> Scafell Pike in the Lake District, at 978 metres, is the highest mountain in England.

England has ten national parks – beautiful areas of countryside where special laws keep the land and the wildlife safe. The biggest of these is the Lake District, in the north-west of England. The Lake District has the highest mountains in the country, with sixteen big lakes lying below them. With its beautiful scenery[85], the Lake District is not surprisingly a very popular place for tourists. Most visitors come to walk in the mountains, to go on boats on the lakes and to enjoy the area's pretty stone-built villages. There is also a lot of wildlife in the Lake District, and it is the only place in the country where golden eagles – birds of prey[86] – live.

In the eighteenth and nineteenth centuries, many poets began to write about the Lake District. The most famous of these was William Wordsworth, who lived there for sixty years. The poems and books that he wrote about the Lake District made many people come and visit the area for the first time.

> **Daffodils**
>
> by William Wordsworth
> (first verse)
>
> I wandered* lonely as a cloud
> That floats* on high o'er* vales* and hills,
> When all at once I saw a crowd,
> A host, of* golden daffodils;
> Beside* the lake, beneath* the trees,
> Fluttering* and dancing in the breeze*.
>
> **wandered** = moved around
> **floats** = sits on water
> **o'er** = over
> **vales** = valleys; low areas between hills
> **a host of** = a lot of
> **beside** = next to
> **beneath** = under
> **fluttering** = moving around quickly, like a bird
> **breeze** = a light wind

Another famous writer from the Lake District is Beatrix Potter, whose children's books about Peter Rabbit and his friends are famous around the world. Today, a lot of tourists visit the house near Hawkshead where she wrote many of her books.

There are four other national parks in the north of England. The Peak District, the Yorkshire Dales and the Northumberland National Park are all part of the Pennines, an area of low mountains in the middle of the north of England. The Pennine Way, a walking trail[87] 429 kilometres long, goes along these mountains, which make a kind of natural border between east and west.

East of the Pennines is the north of England's other national park, the North York Moors, between York in the south and Middlesbrough in

the north. In all these northern national parks, you can find deep valleys covered with forests, high moorland[88] and wonderful caves (natural holes in the rock[89] in the hillside), and they are great places for walking, cycling or horse-riding.

People who have read *Wuthering Heights*, *Jane Eyre*, *The Tenant of Wildfell Hall* or any of the other books by Charlotte, Emily and Anne Brontë, probably feel that they already know the countryside of the Pennines. The Brontë sisters lived in Haworth in Yorkshire, and they describe the windy, heather-covered moorland of this area in many of their books.

> i
> There is a steam railway across the North York Moors. The steam trains from this railway were used as the Hogwarts Express in the *Harry Potter* films.

**The Pennines: countryside of the Brontë sisters**

'I have travelled all over the world, but I am a Yorkshire girl, and I am never happier than when I am walking in the Yorkshire Dales. The beauty and the quiet, the scenery and the food ... I really can't think of anywhere better – well, maybe nowhere better when the sun shines.'

**ELAINE LEMM**

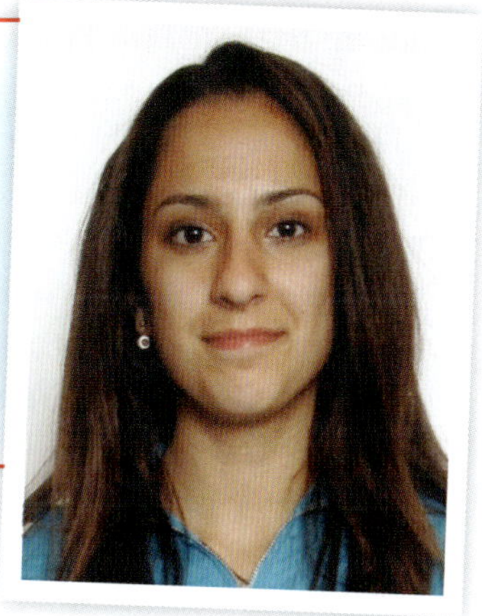

The history of the New Forest, about one hundred kilometres south-west of London, begins more than nine hundred years ago. William the Conqueror wanted this area to be kept for hunting[90], and he and his nobles enjoyed looking for deer and other animals here. Parts of the New Forest, which is now a national park, have probably not changed very much since these times. Today, cows walk freely around this area, with its ancient trees and open land covered with heather. Visitors here can also see beautiful wild flowers, deer and big birds of prey. But most famous are the ponies – about three thousand of them – that live in the New Forest, as they have for many years. You can often see them walking around the villages of the New Forest, and you must be ready to stop your car when one decides to cross the road!

Michael Morpurgo's book *War Horse* is about the adventures of a horse from Devon, and a lot of the film was made in Dartmoor. The director[91] Steven Spielberg said that he had never before had so much natural beauty to film as he found in Dartmoor.

Between Exeter and Plymouth, the national park of Dartmoor in Devon is the biggest and wildest area of open countryside in the south of England. A lot of Dartmoor is moorland and covered in heather, but Dartmoor is also famous for its many tors – hills with rocks at the top. Sheep, cows and ponies walk freely around on Dartmoor, and many birds live here too.

The coast of Exmoor has the highest and lowest tides in Europe. The highest tides here are more than ten metres.

North of Dartmoor is the national park of Exmoor, a beautiful area of moorland, forests, valleys and farmland, which goes across the counties of Somerset and Devon, right up to the coast. Here you can see otters in nearly every river, wild red deer, bats and some very special butterflies.

Devon is not only famous for Dartmoor and Exmoor. The counties of Devon and Cornwall are very popular with tourists because of their lovely countryside and because they get more hours of sunlight than anywhere else in England. Away from the coast, the green fields are full of wild flowers in the summer, and narrow little roads with tall hedges[92] at the side go from one pretty village to the next. By the sea, there are golden beaches and little rocky coves[93], and on the north coast, the big waves[94] in places like Newquay make surfing a very popular sport. Off the coasts of Devon and Cornwall, you can see basking sharks and porpoises, and on Lundy Island there are puffins in April and May.

**Surfing in Newquay, Cornwall**

Another beautiful area to visit in this part of England are the Scilly Isles, about one hundred small islands forty-five kilometres away from Land's End, in England's far south-west corner. Each island is very different, and people live on only five of them.

Along England's south coast, big white cliffs – large rocks next to the sea – look out onto the English Channel. The rocks in the cliffs on part of this coast, which is called the Jurassic Coast and goes from East Devon to Dorset, are one hundred and eighty five million years old. Here you can easily find wonderful fossils – rocks with the shape of animals and plants from ancient times. You can see lots of fossils here because of erosion – the rock is very soft, and every day the sea breaks bits of the rock away from the cliffs. Erosion has made parts of this coast very beautiful: the perfect little cove at Lulworth in Dorset and the famous arch[95] of Durdle Door were both made by erosion.

England's newest national park is the South Downs, which comes down to the sea near Brighton. You can walk through the beautiful green hills of the South Downs on the South Downs Way, a special walking trail which ends at the enormous white cliffs of Beachy Head on the south coast.

Most of the North Sea coast of England (on the east side of the country) is very flat and sandy, with a lot of saltmarsh – wet, muddy areas with grass growing on them. There are many sea birds here and also, at Blakeney Point in Norfolk, several hundred seals. This is the best place in England to see seals, and many people take special boat trips to visit them.

The national park of the Norfolk Broads is also in this area. Here, three rivers go across flat land to the sea, and are so wide in places, they are almost like lakes. Many people like to visit this area by boat or by bike, enjoying the wonderful birdlife.

England has a lot of beautiful countryside, but there are many problems for the environment. Factories, vehicles and modern farming can make the air, rivers and the sea dirty, and this is bad for plants and wildlife. Many animals also lose their homes when forests are cut down or land is taken for building houses on. People believe that global warming (the Earth getting hotter because of dangerous gases in the air) is bringing new problems to the countryside too. It is because of these dangers to the environment that the national parks of England were made, and there are many organizations that work to keep wildlife and the English countryside safe. The UK government is also working with governments from other countries to try to find ways to fight global warming. English people hope that they, and the tourists who come to their country, will always be able to enjoy the wonderful natural environment.

# 6 Daily Life

**English teenagers**

For most English teenagers, daily life is mainly about school. Education is free for all children aged five to sixteen. It is also compulsory – everyone must have an education. As well as state schools, which are run by the government, there are also independent schools, which families have to pay for. About six per cent of children in England go to independent schools. Some families also home-school: they teach their children at home.

Children start their compulsory education in primary school when they are four or five years old, and at age eleven, they move to secondary school. The school year is from September to July, with two-week holidays at Christmas and in the spring, and a longer six-week holiday

English school students often wear a school uniform – usually trousers or a skirt with a shirt and a school jumper, and sometimes a school jacket, called a blazer, and a tie.

'It's half past seven, and I can hear my alarm clock. I go back to sleep, and five minutes later I hear my mum shouting. This time I really have to get up. A quick shower, a piece of toast for breakfast, and I'm ready for school. Well, as ready as I'll ever be.

'At eight fifteen I walk down the road to catch the school bus with my sister Kate. We live in a village in Warwickshire, so we take the bus to our school in Stratford-upon-Avon, half an hour away. If we miss the bus, Mum has to drive us, and then she's late for work. (She's a nurse.)

'School starts at five to nine, and that's when we have to be in our tutor rooms. My tutor's OK. He does the register – calls out everyone's name so he knows who is there. He also helps us with any problems and tells us what's happening at school. I'm in Year 10 now – I'm fifteen – so last year we had to choose our subjects for our GCSE exams next year. I'm doing maths, English, science, art, French, history, geography and media studies. Media studies is all about film, TV, radio, newspapers and magazines – it's my favourite subject. When we hear the bell, we go off for lessons. All my lessons are in different rooms or places around the school and with different teachers. We have two lessons – an hour each – then break, then another two lessons and then lunch. FOOD! I'm always hungry. Some days I bring sandwiches to school, but today I'm eating in the cafeteria – it's like a café, but you wait in a queue[96] and choose what you want. Pizza and salad, not bad. I sit with some friends, and we talk about parents and exams.

'Two more lessons, then at four o'clock the school day is over, but I have school jazz band practice. I play the piano and the saxophone, so music's quite a big part of my life. There's no late school bus, so I walk to my friend Jay's house and wait there until Mum comes to drive me home.

'In the evenings, there's homework and music practice, and I might go to the park and kick a football around with some friends. Watch a bit of TV maybe, go on the computer, phone a few friends, listen to a bit of music. At about ten, Mum tells me to go to sleep, but I'm never ready to. Just like I'm never ready to get up in the morning ...'

**ED MYERS, 15, WARWICKSHIRE**

## English Education

| Primary School | |
|---|---|
| Age 4–5 | Reception |
| Age 5–6 | Year 1 |
| Age 6–7 | Year 2 |
| Age 7–8 | Year 3 |
| Age 8–9 | Year 4 |
| Age 9–10 | Year 5 |
| Age 10–11 | Year 6 |

| Secondary School | |
|---|---|
| Age 11–12 | Year 7 |
| Age 12–13 | Year 8 |
| Age 13–14 | Year 9 |
| Age 14–15 | Year 10 |
| Age 15–16 | Year 11 (GCSEs) |
| Age 16–17 | Year 12 (AS-levels) |
| Age 17–18 | Year 13 (A-levels) |

in the summer. Between each of these holidays, there is a one-week break called Half Term, so the school year has got three terms.

Most state schools follow the national curriculum, which tells teachers what subjects to teach. At the end of Year 11, when students are about sixteen, they take exams called GCSEs in many different subjects. Some of these subjects, such as maths and English, are compulsory, but students can also choose some subjects. After their exams, some students leave education, and others go to technical colleges, where they learn how to do the jobs they are interested in. Others stay at school and study for one or two more years to do exams called AS-levels and A-levels, this time in only three or four subjects. Some students who do well in their A-levels will go on to study at university for another three to six years.

Most jobs in England today are in the service industry – in places like hotels, restaurants, shops, computer companies and banks. Many English people work very hard. The working day is usually from nine o'clock until five o'clock, with an hour at lunchtime, five days a week, but often people work much longer hours.

It can be very difficult for young people to find a job, even if they have studied at university. Some do more training, learning how to do new things. Others take unpaid work, so they can get experience.

In the evenings and at the weekends, many English people enjoy watching or playing sport,

About one in five people in England buy a newspaper every day. There are ten important national newspapers and many regional newspapers – newspapers with local news.

watching TV, playing computer games, or reading books or newspapers. Sometimes they go out to the cinema or to a restaurant, or to see their favourite band play music. Sometimes they just go shopping or spend time with their friends. Children and teenagers often go to weekly clubs, for example Scouts[97], martial arts[98], dance, drama or music. Most teenagers also have a mobile phone, so that they can talk to their friends or send them text messages, and an MP3 player for listening to music.

**Listening to music on an MP3 player**

There are lots of things to do at the weekends and on holidays in England. Many families go out together to museums, beaches or theme parks[99], or for walks or cycle rides in the countryside. People also invite friends to their houses for meals, a cup of tea, or to watch a sports match on TV.

'I really like English people. My favourite things about England are the football, the bands, the literature, movies and the pub culture. On the downside, the food isn't always great, and English people are often too conservative – they don't like change.'

**JOHAN MALMBERG, SWEDEN**

# 6

Life in England is very different if you live in the city or in the countryside. In the city, public transport is usually very good, and there are many buses and trains. London also has an underground train system, called the Tube, and you can travel around Manchester by tram[100]. But in the countryside, people often have to walk and drive a lot.

Seventy-five per cent of England's families have one or more cars.

Most people who live in cities have homes in the suburbs – the areas around a city. Cities often also have big estates. These are places built mainly for people to live in, with lots of houses or flats, and usually some shops and a park. There are lots of different kinds of homes for people to live in in England. Some houses are more than six hundred years old, others are very modern; some people live in houses with several different rooms and a garden, others live in small apartments called flats. In the past, people in England used to buy their own homes, but houses and flats have now become very expensive. For young people with little money, it is now very difficult to buy a home, and more people now rent: they pay money to someone to live in their house or flat.

Most English people usually eat at home because eating out – eating in a restaurant or café – is expensive. Breakfast is often toast or cereal, and while some people have a big meal at midday, others just have a sandwich for lunch and then eat their main meal in the evening. This meal can be called supper, dinner or tea. But for some families, 'tea' is a cup of tea with a biscuit or a piece of cake!

More than fifty per cent of English families have a pet animal. The most popular pets are dogs, cats and rabbits.

Many people now buy their food and all the other shopping they need from big supermarkets, which are on the outside of almost every town and city. These supermarkets are often open all day and in the evening, and some now stay open all night too. Other shops usually open at nine o'clock and close at half-past five or six, with shorter opening hours on Sundays.

Life in England is busier than ever today. Travel around any English city at rush hour – when people are going to or from work – and it seems that no one has time for anything. But over a morning coffee or the important afternoon cup of tea, most English people can always find the time to talk about sport or the weather, or think of something to laugh about.

Shopping in an English town

# 7 Sports

**The Olympic® stadium, London**

Sport is very important in England, and people enjoy going to big sports events or watching them on TV and playing sport in their free time. Some of the most popular world sports – football, rugby, cricket, golf and tennis – first started in England, and people from all around the world come here for some of its great sports events.

In 2012, the Olympics were held in England, and millions of people from around the world came to London to watch the many different sports of the Olympics and the Paralympics. New sports stadiums were built, including the main Olympic stadium, a basketball arena[101] and a velopark, for cycling. It was the first time the Olympics had come to England since 1948 and was a very exciting year for the country.

The most popular sport in England is football, and there are professional matches every week from August until May. Many thousands of people also play in parks, at local clubs, and at schools or universities. Football has been played in England for hundreds of years, and the best football teams, for example Manchester United, Liverpool, Chelsea and Arsenal, are famous around the world. The most important day in England's football calendar is the Football Association (FA) Cup Final day in May at London's Wembley Stadium.

Many people believe that England's best ever footballer was Bobby Charlton, who started playing for Manchester United in 1953 and scored 249 goals over the next twenty years. In 1958, Charlton was in an aeroplane with the Manchester United team when it crashed, killing eight players. Bobby Charlton was not killed in the crash, and he went on to play in the 1966 World Cup, which England won. It was the first and only time that England has won the World Cup.

Cricket was first played in England in the sixteenth century, and by the eighteenth century, it had become the country's national sport. Every summer, teams from other countries play five-day Test matches against the English national team. Cricket is also played on village greens – small fields in villages – around the country in the summer months. Because cricket matches are so long, a new kind of match called the Twenty20 was introduced in 2003. Twenty20 matches are only three hours long, so people can watch them in one day.

**A cricket match on the village green**

> The winner's cup for the Rugby Union World Cup Final is called the William Webb Ellis Cup. People say that William Webb Ellis, a student at Rugby School, introduced the game of rugby when he picked up the ball during a game of football.

Rugby is another sport that began in England, and it is named after the school where it was first played – Rugby School in Warwickshire. Rugby is like football, but players can hold the ball and tackle each other – pull each other to the ground – to get the ball. Rugby is not as popular as football, but after England won the World Cup in 2003, more people began to watch and play the sport. In England, there are two kinds of rugby, each very different: Rugby League and Rugby Union.

> Traditionally, when people visit Wimbledon for the tennis, they eat strawberries and cream.

For two weeks around the end of June, England becomes tennis-mad! This is the time of the Wimbledon Championships, the most famous tennis tournament in the world. Few people watch tennis on TV for the rest of the year, but during Wimbledon, matches are shown on TV every afternoon and evening.

England's most famous tennis player was Fred Perry, who won the Wimbledon Championship every year for three years, from 1934 to 1936. Since that time, no English player has won the Men's Championship.

Horse-racing is another very popular sport in England. There are races every day of the year, and people enjoy making bets[102] on which horse will win. The Derby at Epsom, which continues to be held today, was the first derby ever, and derbies – races on flat ground for three-year-old horses – are now held around the world. Other important dates in horse-racing are the Grand National in Liverpool in April – one of the most difficult horse races in the world – and Royal Ascot, five days of horse racing in Berkshire in June. The Queen always goes to Ascot, so it is an important event in England, and visitors wear their best clothes and hats.

Another important day for sport in England is the London Marathon in April. More than thirty thousand people run in the London Marathon, which has been held since 1981. The fastest people finish the forty-two-kilometre run in just over two hours, but for many runners the most important thing is making money for charity[103].

The London Marathon

Watersports are popular in England, and many people, especially on the south coast, enjoy sailing. There are good waves for surfing at many of the beaches in the south-west, and canoeing is also popular on England's many rivers and canals. Two of England's most famous sportspeople do a watersport – Steve Redgrave, who won gold medals for rowing at every Olympic Games between 1984 and 2000, and Ellen MacArthur, who broke the world record for sailing around the world alone in the fastest time on 7th February 2005.

Golf is also a very popular sport for English people. There are many golf courses in England, and every July the Open Championship, one of the four biggest tournaments in the world, is held in England or Scotland.

Motor-racing is also well-liked, and many people go to a course called Silverstone in Northamptonshire every year to watch the British Grand Prix.

At school, children play football, rugby, netball and cricket, and do athletics in the summer. There are public swimming pools and gyms in most towns, and many people also enjoy cycling and walking. Other outdoor activities like mountaineering – climbing and walking in the hills and mountains – are also very popular in England.

English people love sport. For some time, they have not won many big events in the sports that first came from their country many years before. But sport continues to be a very important part of life in England.

> George Mallory was an English mountaineer who tried three times to climb Mount Everest. The third time, in 1924, he died a few hundred metres from the top of the mountain. No one knows if he died on his way up Everest or on his way down, so it is possible that he was the first person to climb the highest mountain in the world.

# 8 Entertainment

**The Queen's Theatre, London**

England is famous around the world for its great culture and entertainment. Some of the world's greatest writers, best films, and most famous actors and directors have come from England, and there are several hundred theatres and concert halls[104] showing wonderful plays, music and dance.

Literature is a very important part of England's history, and all around the country you can visit the homes of some of the many great English writers. The most famous of these is, of course, William Shakespeare, but many others have written great works of literature too. In the late seventeenth century, there were some fine poets, for example John Milton, who wrote *Paradise Lost*. Novels only began to be widely written in the eighteenth century, and one of the earliest of these was Daniel Defoe's *Robinson Crusoe*, published[105] in 1719, which continues to be very popular today.

The first half of the nineteenth century was famous for the Romantic poetry of writers like Wordsworth, Coleridge, Byron, Shelley and Keats. Jane Austen was another great writer of this time. In books like *Emma*, *Pride and Prejudice* and *Persuasion*, Austen wrote about how women saw society, marriage and happiness.

Famous Victorian writers included Charles Dickens, the Brontë sisters and George Eliot. In Victorian times, people began for the first time to write literature just for children, and one of the best-known of these new children's books was Lewis Carroll's *Alice's Adventures in Wonderland*, which continues to be read by many children even today.

Another writer from around this time whose work is much-loved now is Arthur Conan Doyle, who was Scottish. He wrote stories about Sherlock Holmes, a London detective, between 1880 and 1907. Sherlock Holmes had a brilliant mind and was able to find the answers to the strangest mysteries. The stories of these mysteries were told to the reader by Sherlock Holmes's great friend Dr Watson.

An important English writer at the beginning of the twentieth century was Thomas Hardy. *Tess of the d'Urbervilles*, *Far From the Madding Crowd* and Hardy's other novels were often terribly sad stories about people in an imaginary[106] county called Wessex. Rudyard Kipling was also popular at this time and from 1910, a new kind of 'modernist' literature became important. One of the first modernist writers was Joseph Conrad, who was Polish, but lived in England, and between the two wars there was a lot of other new literature, from writers like Virginia Woolf, Evelyn Waugh and DH Lawrence.

After the Second World War, two of England's most important writers were George Orwell, who wrote *Nineteen Eighty-Four* and *Animal Farm*, and Agatha Christie, who wrote sixty-six detective novels, including the adventures of Miss Marple and Hercule Poirot. Modern fantasy literature – writing about magic[107], monsters and other imaginary things – became popular at this time too, when *The Lord of the Rings*, by JRR Tolkien, was published in 1949.

Two of the most famous writers of the last fifty years are children's writers. Roald Dahl, who was born in Wales to Norwegian parents, wrote books such as *Charlie and the Chocolate Factory* and *Matilda*, many of which also

People queuing to buy *Harry Potter* books

When the last book in the *Harry Potter* series was published in 2007, some people queued for more than two days outside bookshops to buy the first copies.

became great films and theatre shows. JK Rowling's *Harry Potter* series – a group of seven fantasy books for children – has sold hundreds of millions of copies, and people can now read them in sixty-seven different languages.

Many of these works of literature have become famous plays, and for many people an important part of any visit to England is a trip to the theatre. There are several hundred theatres in England, around the country, but the most famous are the theatres of the West End in London. In the West End, there is a theatre on nearly every street, showing the latest plays and musicals[108], and many of the best actors from all around the world come to perform here. Some of the most famous shows in the West End have been musicals, such as *Cats* and *Phantom of the Opera* by Andrew Lloyd Webber, but in London and around the country, you can also see many different kinds of shows, including more serious plays, new works and comedy.

One of the oldest theatres in London is the Old Vic, which first began to show plays in 1818. England also has the National Theatre, on London's South Bank near the London Eye, which opened in 1976. Across the Thames are the Royal Ballet and the Royal Opera House at Covent Garden, and the English National Opera at the Coliseum, the largest theatre in London.

Outside London, England's most famous theatre is the theatre of the Royal Shakespeare Company in Stratford-upon-Avon, where Shakespeare's plays are performed throughout the year. In the summer, you can also see Shakespeare's plays at the Globe Theatre in London, a round theatre with no roof, like the one where these famous plays were first performed more than four hundred years ago.

England is important for its music too. George Frideric Handel, Edward Elgar and Gustav Holst are three of the country's most famous classical music[109] composers, and at places like the Royal Festival Hall and the Barbican Centre in London, you can hear many different kinds of classical music, played by some of the finest orchestras in the world. There is also a lot of good classical music outside London: the Birmingham Symphony Orchestra is one of the best in Europe, and at many stately homes and castles around the country there are outdoor concerts in the summer.

But it is for its pop music that England is best known. Together with the USA, the UK brought rock 'n' roll to the world in the 1950s, and The Beatles, who became popular in the 1960s, is one of the most famous bands in the world. During the 1960s, the Rolling Stones, Cliff Richard and The

**The Beatles**

Shadows, The Who, The Kinks, The Animals and many other bands became important in England, and they started to become famous in the USA too. For a while, the USA began to follow the UK in music and in fashion.

In the 1970s, music changed. First there was glam rock from artists like David Bowie and Elton John, who coloured their hair, and wore strange and wonderful clothes and shoes. Then came punk rock – short, fast songs, often with a political message, sung by bands like the Clash. In the 1980s, world music, heavy metal (loud, hard music) and indie rock were popular, and England's dance music culture also began. But in the late 1990s, some artists turned against the many fashions in music of the '80s and early '90s, and Britpop arrived – bands such as Blur, Oasis and Radiohead that followed the British guitar music of the 1960s and '70s. Several of these bands became famous around Europe and in the USA.

Today, you can see bands play in clubs in almost every big city, and there are also music festivals around the country where people camp and watch music in big fields. The most famous of these is at Glastonbury.

Art-lovers can find a lot to enjoy in England too. Two of England's most famous artists were the landscape painters John Constable and JMW Turner, and many of their pictures can be seen at the Tate Britain gallery in London. London also has the Tate Modern, of course, and there are also great exhibitions[110] at the Royal Academy of Arts, and a lot of Western European art at the National Gallery in Trafalgar Square. In the 1990s, a group of artists called the Young British Artists (YBAs) became very popular in England. One of the most famous YBAs was Damien Hirst, who made a lot of art works with dead animals. Some people love his work, and others hate it!

Most towns in England have a cinema, and watching films is a very popular activity for English people. England has made some of the world's greatest films, and some of the most famous actors and directors are English.

The film industry only really started in England in the 1930s, when some famous films like *The 39 Steps* were made. But it was in the 1950s and 1960s that British cinema became really important. At this time, Hammer Horror films like *The Curse of Frankenstein* and *Dracula* were made – and Ealing Comedies like *Kind Hearts and Coronets* and *Whisky Galore*. The first *Carry On* film was made in 1958, and by 1992, there were thirty-one. The *Carry On* films were comedies that made jokes about English life. They were not thought of as important films, but were loved by many English people.

The James Bond films were another series that became very famous in England. The stories were adventures about James Bond, a secret service agent – someone who worked secretly for the government, looking for enemies of the country. The first Bond film, *Dr No*, was made in 1962, and the films became famous for their music, Bond's cars and clever equipment, and for James Bond himself – a character played by several different actors.

A famous English actor of the 1960s was Julie Andrews, who appeared in two famous musical films, *The Sound of Music* and *Mary Poppins*. But many people believe that the greatest actor of the twentieth century was Laurence Olivier. Olivier, who worked in theatre and film from the 1920s until the 1980s, made nearly sixty films, including *Rebecca* and *Wuthering Heights*.

Also very famous, but as a director not an actor, was Alfred Hitchcock. He made many great mystery films in England and in Hollywood, where he later went to live.

The first English film with sound was *Blackmail*, directed by Alfred Hitchcock in 1929.

**Laurence Olivier, in *Rebecca***

From the 1990s, romantic comedies like *Four Weddings and a Funeral* and *Notting Hill* were made, and the Merchant Ivory films of classic novels like *Howard's End*. Since then, some of England's most successful films have been *Love Actually*, *Slumdog Millionaire* and the *Harry Potter* series.

But England's most popular kind of entertainment is television. Public television first began in England in 1936, and the British Broadcasting Corporation (the BBC) is the world's oldest and largest broadcaster[111]. Today

there are five main channels in England, and there are also hundreds more channels on cable and satellite TV. There are hundreds of radio stations too.

The children's programme *Blue Peter* has been on TV since 1958.

On English TV, there are many different kinds of programmes, but some of the most popular ones are sitcoms (situation comedies) – comedies about people in their home or where they work. One of the most famous of these was *Fawlty Towers*, with the actor John Cleese. Many people also enjoy soap operas – dramas which continue from one programme to the next, for example *Eastenders*, *Coronation Street*, *Emmerdale* and *Hollyoaks*. Another very popular drama series in England in the 1990s was *Inspector Morse*, about a detective in Oxford.

Ninety-six per cent of people in England have TVs in their homes, and most English people watch about twenty-five hours a week of TV.

Many people also enjoy reality programmes – programmes about ordinary people's lives. One of the most famous of these is *Big Brother*, a programme in which a group of people live together in a house and are filmed twenty-four hours a day. Some of the *Big Brother* programmes have been watched by up to six million people in the UK: England has great music, art, history and literature, but sometimes people are most interested in day-to-day life!

**Television**

# 9 English Heroes

**William Shakespeare**

Who are England's heroes – the important people who will never be forgotten? One of the greatest must be William Shakespeare, who wrote many beautiful poems and about thirty-seven plays, including *A Midsummer Night's Dream*, *Romeo and Juliet*, *Hamlet* and *Macbeth*. The people in his plays always seem very real, and he wrote about their feelings and problems in words that continue to sound new and interesting today.

Another hero of England from the world of literature is Charles Dickens. Dickens wrote some of the best novels of Victorian times, including *Oliver Twist*, *David Copperfield*, *Bleak House* and *Little Dorrit*. Dickens used his books to show how terrible life was for poor people in England at the time of the industrial revolution.

Many phrases from William Shakespeare's writing are used today. Match the phrases with their meanings.

1 All's well that ends well.
2 Love is blind.
3 Too much of a good thing.
4 Off with his head.
5 More fool you.

a Cut off his head.
b When you are in love, you don't see the bad things about someone.
c It is OK to try something if it works out well in the end.
d How silly you are!
e Having too much of something can be bad.

But England has scientific heroes as well as heroes from the world of literature. One of the greatest of these was Sir Isaac Newton. Born in Lincolnshire in 1643, Newton studied at the University of Cambridge. He was able to understand and explain many things about the world around us for the first time, and his book *Mathematical Principles of Natural Philosophy* was very important in the history of science. Newton helped people to understand about light and colour, and he was also the first person to explain gravity – the force that pulls things towards the ground.

Charles Darwin also did scientific work in England. He was born into a rich family, and in 1831 he left England to travel around the world. Darwin studied the animals and plants that he saw on his trip, and was interested in the differences between them. When he came home, he began to work on a new idea: the theory of evolution. This was the idea that only the strongest animals and plants lived and reproduced – had babies or grew seeds. And so, Darwin believed, each kind of animal and plant was slowly changing. In 1859, Darwin published his ideas in the book *On the Origin of Species*.

One very real hero of England was Horatio Nelson, who was leader of the Royal Navy[112] from 1794 to 1805. Nelson, who lost one eye and one arm in battle, was a great leader, and with him, Britain won many battles against France during the Napoleonic Wars. At the Battle of Trafalgar, Nelson helped to stop the French from invading Britain, but he was then killed. A very large statue of him stands forty-six metres high in Trafalgar Square and is one of London's best-loved sights.

Two other important English seamen were Sir Francis Drake and Captain Cook. Sir Francis Drake helped to lead England against the Spanish Armada in 1588, and Captain Cook was the first European to reach the east coast of Australia, in 1770.

Nelson's Column

Winston Churchill, prime minister from 1940 until 1945, was another English hero for many people during World War Two. Churchill was a strong leader, and many people believe that the speeches and radio broadcasts he made during the war helped the UK to win the war. He was prime minister again from 1951 to 1955, and when he died in 1965, the Queen gave him a state funeral[113] – a special funeral that is normally only for kings and queens.

> *Courage[114] is what it takes to stand up and speak; courage is also what it takes to sit down and listen.*

**Winston Churchill, prime minister 1940–45, 1951–55**

Another famous politician was Margaret Thatcher. Thatcher was prime minister from 1979 to 1990 – longer than any other person in the twentieth century – and she was also the first woman prime minister of the UK.

One of England's most famous heroes is not actually real. Stories about Robin Hood have been popular since the Middle Ages, and in modern times many films, plays and TV programmes have been made about him. In these old stories, Robin Hood is a great fighter and an outlaw – someone who does not follow the law. Living in Sherwood Forest at a time when the king of England is a dishonest man, he takes money from the rich to give it to the poor.

Florence Nightingale was famous for helping people too – but she was a real person. Florence Nightingale is thought of by many as the first real nurse. In 1854, during the Crimean War, she went to work in a hospital for soldiers. She thought that it was dirty and badly organized, so she quickly started to make important changes. Because of her, the hospital became cleaner, the soldiers were given good food and taken care of better, and soon fewer people were dying. When she came back to England, Florence Nightingale started the first proper nursing school at St Thomas' Hospital.

> i
>
> Florence Nightingale was called the 'Lady with the Lamp' in the Crimean War because every night she walked around the hospital to visit the sick soldiers.

England also has heroes of the stage and screen. One of the first of these was Charlie Chaplin, a comedy actor and director who was famous for his many silent films in the years before films with sound were made. Chaplin's best-known character was 'The Tramp', a funny little man with a hat, a moustache[115] and a stick. Before the end of the First World War, Chaplin was the most famous film actor in the world.

But probably the greatest stage heroes of England are The Beatles. John Lennon, Paul McCartney, George Harrison and Ringo Starr had their first hit[116], *Love Me Do*, in 1962, and by 1964, they had become famous around the world. There was international 'Beatlemania': people screamed and shouted when the band came on stage, and the world watched everything they did. The Beatles were the first English band to become successful in the USA. They made more than two hundred songs and are the best-selling band in history.

Two more musical heroes of England, famous in a quieter way, are the composers George Frideric Handel and Sir Edward Elgar. Handel was German, but came to live in London in 1712 and became British in 1727. He is one of the greatest composers in history and is best known for wonderful works like *Water Music* and *The Messiah*, written in 1742. Elgar's most famous works are the *Enigma Variations*, written in 1899, *The Dream of Gerontius* and the *Pomp and Circumstance Marches*.

What about modern-day English heroes? For many football lovers, David Beckham is a hero. He was captain of the England football team from 2000 until 2006 and, along with his wife Victoria, who was once in the band the Spice Girls, Beckham is a very famous celebrity.

Princess Diana is also, for many people, an English hero. Diana was the first wife of Charles, the Prince of Wales, and when they married in 1981, people believed that she would one day be the queen. But they were not happy together, and in 1996 Charles and Diana ended their marriage. A year later, Diana was killed in a car accident in Paris. Many people loved her for her work with international charities and because she showed great kindness to children, ill people and those with difficult lives. When she died, thousands of people brought flowers to her London home, and two-and-a-half billion people watched her funeral on TV.

**Princess Diana**

# 10 Looking Forward

**Tim Berners-Lee, inventor of the World Wide Web**

All through England's history, small inventions – new things that people make – have brought big changes to people's lives. When William Caxton made the first English printing press[117] in 1476, the country changed in many ways. Now people could get more books, more cheaply, and so they could get information about lots of different things. Because of this, information also became more standardized: it was written down in the same way each time, which was important in areas like science. The printing press changed the English language too. At that time, people in different parts of the country used very different words, but William Caxton only printed books in standardized English.

The spinning Jenny, invented in 1764 by James Hargreaves, brought more important changes to England. With the spinning Jenny, people working in their homes in England could spin[118] cotton more quickly and so make much more. Other machines followed, and when steam power was introduced, cloth-making became a proper industry. Cloth-makers did not work at home anymore; they used big machines in factories in the cities.

This was the beginning of the industrial revolution, and in twenty-first century England, people are in the middle of another revolution, or great change, again started by several small inventions.

One of the most important of these was the invention by the Englishman Tim Berners-Lee, in 1990, of the World Wide Web[119]. The World Wide Web has made it easier than ever for people to get information. Its invention is part of the digital revolution[120], which has given us mobile phones, computers, MP3 players, digital TV and much, much more.

**The digital world**

> Seventy-six per cent of homes in England use the Internet, and nine out of ten English people have a mobile phone.

The digital revolution is changing many things about life in England. We can now talk on the telephone almost anywhere, send messages quickly around the world and see people who are thousands of kilometres away through our computers. Because of this, people can study or work from home more easily, and work with people in different countries. We can shop and meet people on the Internet,

read books on our computers and watch hundreds of different TV channels. And the machines we use every day, like radios, washing machines and cameras, are becoming better and cheaper all the time.

But the digital revolution is also bringing new problems. Many people feel that modern technology makes life busier and sometimes more difficult. We can work wherever we are now, so for some people there is less time to think or to relax. Is it good for children to play computer games and watch TV so much? And are we forgetting how to meet people and make real friends because we talk to people through computers so much now?

These are all difficult questions for England's future, and there are other questions we are trying to answer now too. For a long time, we have known that there are big environmental problems in the world. Factories, cars, and burning coal, oil or gas for fuel all make our air dirty, giving us global warming. So now we need to find ways to help the environment.

Many English homes and companies are already getting their electricity from solar (sun) or wind power, and the government is giving money to people who use these renewable energies – ones that can be used again and again. In the future, we will probably use less and less coal, oil and gas. Many English people have been recycling[121] more and more of their rubbish, and by 2011, they were recycling forty per cent of their rubbish. In the future, many people also believe that we will use electric cars more and other energy-saving technologies.

**Using wind power to make electricity**

The digital and environmental revolutions are changing England. England in 2100 will be a very different place to the England we now know. Will England have a king or queen? Will there continue to be big differences between rich and poor people? How many different languages will people speak? And will England have won the Football World Cup again? We cannot know. But we can probably hope that people will continue to watch Shakespeare's plays, climb the mountains of the Lake District and visit the sights of London. And perhaps they will still say that England is a wonderful, exciting place.

# Points For Understanding

## 1

1 When did the Romans live in England?

2 In the famous story about King Arthur, how did people know that Arthur should be the next king of England?

3 What were the seven kingdoms of England in the Anglo-Saxon period?

4 Was the English town Worcester a Roman town, an Anglo-Saxon town or a Viking town?

5 Who became the king of England after the Battle of Hastings?

6 What important change did Henry the Eighth make to religion in England?

7 Why was the period 1649 to 1660 very unusual in England's history?

8 How did the industrial revolution change Britain?

9 What happened when Britain lost the American War of Independence?

## 2

1 Who were the suffragettes?

2 How did the First World War change life for women?

3 In what way was the Second World War different from the First World War?

4 Why did many colonies become independent after the Second World War?

5 Why did many people in the UK buy TVs in 1952?

6 What things show us that England is a very multicultural country now?

## 3

1 For which festival do English people eat turkey and cranberry sauce?

2 What do people do on April Fool's Day?

3 In the past, what three important foods did people give up eating for Lent, and what do English people make with them?

4 What do people give each other at Easter?

5 Why do people wear poppies on Remembrance Day?

6 Name three royal traditions.

7 What is a traditional Sunday lunch?

## 4

1 In which areas of London can you find:
   - a the Houses of Parliament?
   - b theatres, restaurants, cinemas and clubs?
   - c street entertainers and an old market?
   - d big banks and St Paul's Cathedral?

2 In which English city can you find:
   - a the National Railway Museum?
   - b The Royal Pavilion?
   - c England's oldest university?
   - d the National Exhibition Centre?
   - e the Clifton Suspension Bridge?
   - f pottery factories?
   - g famous Roman baths?

3 What can tourists do in Liverpool?

4 What is the *Angel of the North*?

5 Why is Stonehenge one of the wonders of the world?

6 What is *The Canterbury Tales*?

## 5

1 What are England's ten national parks?

2 Name two famous writers from the Lake District.

3 Where can you take the steam train that was the Hogwarts Express in the *Harry Potter* films?

4 Which famous writer sisters lived in the Pennines?

5 Name four kinds of animals you can find in the New Forest.

6 Where is the best place in England to look for fossils?

7 Where is the best place in England to see seals?

## 6

1 What is the difference between a state school and an independent school in England?

2 What is the national curriculum?

3 Name three things English families like to do at the weekends and on holidays.

4 What percentage of England's families have a car?

5 When are English supermarkets open?

## 7

1 Name five sports that first started in England.

2 Why were 2012, 1966 and 2003 exciting years for sport in England?

3 What is the most popular sport in England?

4 Why was Twenty20 cricket introduced in 2003?

5 Who introduced the game of rugby, and how?

6 What is England's most famous tennis tournament?

7 What sport is Ellen MacArthur famous for?

8 What sport can you watch at Silverstone in Northamptonshire?

## 8

1 Name three famous English children's writers.

2 Where is the most important area for theatres in London?

3 What was the most famous music style of the 1990s in England?

4 Why are James Bond films famous?

5 When did public television first begin in England?

## 9

1 What did Charles Dickens write about in his novels?

2 What did Sir Isaac Newton teach people?

3 What was Charles Darwin's theory of evolution?

4 Where can you see a statue of Horatio Nelson?

5 Who was Winston Churchill?

6 Who was the first woman prime minister of the UK?

7 Who was Florence Nightingale?

8 Why did many people love Princess Diana?

## 10

1 What did William Caxton, James Hargreaves and Tim Berners-Lee invent?

2 What percentage of English homes use the Internet?

3 What are the possible problems of modern technology?

4 How are people in England trying to help the environment?

5 What percentage of rubbish is recycled in England?

# Glossary

1 ***society*** (page 5)
people living together in organized communities, with laws and traditions controlling the way that they behave towards each other

2 ***parliament*** (page 5)
an official elected group of people who meet to make the laws of the country and discuss national issues. These people, who control the country and make decisions about its laws and taxes, are known as the *government*.

3 ***led*** – *to lead something* (page 5)
to be in charge of an organization, group of people or activity. Someone who leads a group, organization or country is called a *leader*.

4 ***mud*** (page 7)
very soft, wet earth

5 ***invaded*** – *to invade somewhere* (page 7)
to take or send an army into another country in order to get control of it

6 ***weapon*** (page 7)
an object that can be used for hurting people or damaging property, for example a gun, knife or bomb

7 ***battle*** (page 7)
a fight between two armies in a war

8 ***controlled*** – *to control something* (page 7)
to have the power to make decisions about what happens in a place or situation

9 ***religion*** (page 7)
belief in a god or in gods, or a particular system of beliefs in a god or in gods

10 ***literature*** (page 8)
stories and other types of writing, especially those that are considered to have value as art. Types of *literature* include *poetry* or *poems* – pieces of writing that use beautiful or unusual language. They are arranged in lines that have a particular regular sound, and the lines often end with a similar sound. *Plays* are another type of literature. A *play* is a piece of writing that is intended to be performed by actors in a theatre, or on TV or the radio.

11 ***sword*** (page 8)
a weapon with a short handle and a long, sharp *blade* – the thin, sharp part of a knife, tool or weapon

12 ***defeated*** – *to defeat someone* (page 8)
to win against someone in a fight or competition

13 ***powerful*** (page 10)
able to influence or control what people do or think

14 ***conqueror*** (page 10)
someone who has taken control of land or people by force

15 ***competition*** (page 11)
an organized event in which people try to win prizes by being better than other people. A *tournament* is a type of competition in which people play a series of games. The winner of each game plays in the next game until there is only one person or team left.

16 ***power*** (page 13)
political control of a country or government

17 ***civil war*** (page 13)
a war that is fought between different groups of people within the same country

18 ***cloth*** (page 13)
material used for making things such as clothes and curtains

19 ***coal*** (page 13)
a hard, black substance that is dug from the ground and burned as *fuel* – a substance that produces heat or power when it is burned

20 ***iron*** (page 13)
a hard, heavy metal that is used for making steel

21 ***industry*** (page 13)
a business involved in producing a particular type of goods or services

22 ***steam engine*** (page 14)
a machine that produces movement, for example in a vehicle like a train or car. It gets its power from *steam* – the power that is created when water is heated.

23 ***independent*** (page 14)
not controlled by another country or organization

24 ***empire*** (page 14)
a number of countries that are ruled by one person or government

25 ***factory*** (page 15)
a building where large quantities of goods are produced using machines

26 ***rubbish*** (page 15)
things that you throw away because they are no longer useful

27 ***sank*** – *to sink* (page 16)
to disappear below the surface of water, or to make something do this

28 ***vote*** – *to vote* (page 16)
to choose a representative by officially stating your choice in an election

29 ***march*** (page 16)
a walk by a group of people to a place in order to protest about something

30 ***race*** (page 17)
a competition that decides who is the fastest at doing something

31 ***ally*** (page 17)
a country that makes an agreement to help another country, especially in a war

32 ***political*** (page 17)
relating to politics – the ideas and activities that are involved in getting power in an area or governing it. A *political party* is an organized group of people who share the same ideas about how a country should be governed, and who try to get elected.

33 ***depression*** (page 17)
a period of time when there is a lot of unemployment and a lot of people are poor because there is very little economic activity

34 ***price*** (page 17)
the amount of money that you have to pay in order to buy something

35 ***bomb*** (page 17)
a weapon that is made to explode at a particular time or when it hits something

36 ***education*** (page 18)
the activity of teaching people in schools, colleges and universities, and all the policies and arrangements concerning this

37 ***immigrant*** (page 19)
someone who comes to live in a country from another country

38 ***coronation*** (page 19)
a ceremony at which someone officially becomes a king or queen

39 ***multicultural*** (page 20)
consisting of people of different cultures

40 ***enthusiastic*** (page 22)
very interested in something, or excited by it

41 ***turkey*** (page 22)
the meat from a large bird that is similar to a chicken. *Turkey* is usually eaten with *cranberry sauce* – a liquid food made from a small, sour, red fruit. This meat is often eaten with *Brussels sprouts* – a small, round vegetable consisting of many green leaves which is also popular at Christmas.

42 ***decorate*** – *to decorate something* (page 23)
to make something more attractive by putting nice things on it or in it

43 ***strike*** – *to strike (something)* (page 23)
if a clock strikes, or if it strikes a particular time, it makes a sound to show what the time is

44 ***firework*** (page 23)
an object that makes loud noises and coloured lights in the sky when it explodes

45 ***celebration*** (page 23)
a special or important time or event

46 ***spaghetti*** (page 24)
a type of pasta – an Italian food made from flour and water, and sometimes eggs – that is in the form of long, thin pieces like string

47 ***pancake*** (page 24)
a thin, round, flat food made by cooking a mixture of flour, eggs and milk

48 ***frying pan*** (page 24)
a flat metal pan with a long handle that is used for cooking food in hot oil or fat

49 ***whisk*** – *to whisk something* (page 24)
to mix something such as eggs or cream using a *whisk* – a kitchen tool that consists of several curves of wire joined to a handle

50 ***melt*** – *to melt something* (page 24)
to change a solid substance into a liquid

51 ***pole*** (page 25)
a long, thin stick, often used for holding or supporting something

52 ***ribbon*** (page 25)
a long, narrow piece of coloured cloth or paper that is used for decorating or tying things

53 ***blow up*** – *to blow (something) up* (page 25)
if something blows up, or if someone blows something up, it explodes and is destroyed

54 ***treating*** – *to treat someone* (page 25)
to behave towards someone in a particular way

55 ***bonfire*** (page 25)
a large fire built outside for burning rubbish or for a celebration

56 ***royal*** (page 25)
relating to a king or queen, or to their family

57 ***carriage*** (page 25)
a vehicle pulled by horses, used in the past for carrying passengers

58 ***speech*** (page 25)
a formal occasion when someone speaks to an audience, or the words that someone speaks to an audience

59 ***guarding*** – *to guard something* (page 26)
to protect someone or something from danger or harm

60 ***bearskin*** (page 26)
the skin and fur of a *bear* – a large wild animal with thick fur

61 ***vinegar*** (page 27)
a sour liquid that is used for adding flavour to food

62 ***sausage*** (page 28)
a food that consists of a long, thin tube of skin containing meat mixed with spices

63 *carry – to carry something* (page 28)
to hold someone or something using your hands, arms or body and take them somewhere

64 ***fair*** (page 29)
an outdoor event with goods for sale and competitions, usually organized by a school or church to make money or as a celebration

65 ***costume*** (page 29)
clothes that are typical of a particular place or period in history

66 ***architect*** (page 31)
someone whose job is to design buildings

67 ***museum*** (page 32)
a building where valuable and important objects are kept for people to see and study

68 ***Ferris wheel*** (page 32)
a machine, usually at a fair or park, in the shape of a large wheel with seats on the edge, that takes people round and round in the air

69 ***dungeon*** (page 32)
a dark underground room in a castle that was used as a prison in the past

70 ***event*** (page 33)
an organized occasion such as a concert or sports competition

71 ***band*** (page 34)
a group of musicians who play popular music

72 ***pier*** (page 35)
a structure that is built out from the land over water. It is used for getting on and off boats, fishing, walking, etc, and for entertainment.

73 ***amusement arcade*** (page 35)
a place where you can play games on machines by putting coins in them

74 ***sculpture*** (page 35)
a solid object that someone makes as a work of art by shaping a substance such as stone, metal or wood

75 ***angel*** (page 35)
a spirit that in some religions is believed to live in heaven with God. In pictures, angels are shown as beautiful people with wings.

76 ***mine*** (page 35)
a large hole or tunnel made in the ground from which people take coal, gold, etc

77 ***border*** (page 36)
the official line that separates two countries or regions

78 ***port*** (page 36)
a town or city on the coast with an area of water where ships stop

79 ***electronics*** (page 36)
the science and technology of equipment that uses electricity and extremely small electrical parts such as microchips

80 ***engineer*** (page 36)
someone who designs things such as roads, railways or machines

81 ***pyramid*** (page 37)
a large, pointed stone structure with a square base and triangular sides

82 ***ancient*** (page 37)
relating to a period of history a very long time ago

83 ***rainforest*** (page 37)
a forest in a tropical region of the world where it rains a lot

84 ***wildlife*** (page 39)
animals, birds and plants that live in natural conditions

85 ***scenery*** (page 41)
natural things such as trees, hills and lakes that you can see in a particular place

86 ***bird of prey*** (page 41)
a bird that hunts and eats other animals

87 ***trail*** (page 41)
a path through the countryside, especially one designed for walking for pleasure

88 ***moorland*** (page 42)
a large area of high land that is covered with grass, bushes and a small plant with white and purple flowers called heather, and has soil that is not good for growing crops

89 ***rock*** (page 42)
a large piece of the solid substance that forms part of the Earth's surface

90 ***hunting*** (page 43)
the activity of catching and killing wild animals

91 ***director*** (page 43)
someone whose job is to tell the actors and technical staff who are involved in a film, play or programme what to do

92 ***hedge*** (page 44)
a line of bushes or small trees that are growing close together around a garden or a field

93 ***cove*** (page 44)
a small area of sea that is partly surrounded by land

94 ***wave*** (page 44)
a line of water that rises up on the surface of a sea, lake or river. The big *waves* on the sea in Devon and Cornwall are perfect for *surfing* – a sport in which people ride on waves using surfboards.

95 ***arch*** (page 45)
a shape or structure with straight sides and a curved top. The curved top part is also called an *arch*.

96 ***queue*** (page 47)
a line of people that are waiting for something

97 ***Scouts*** (page 49)
The Scout Association – an organization that encourages young people aged six to twenty-five to learn practical skills and help other people

98 ***martial art*** (page 49)
a sport that is a traditional Asian form of fighting such as karate or judo

99 ***theme park*** (page 49)
a large park where people pay to play games and have fun and where all the entertainment is designed according to one *theme* – the main subject of something

100 ***tram*** (page 50)
a long, narrow vehicle for carrying passengers that travels along metal tracks in the middle of a street

101 ***arena*** (page 52)
a large area surrounded by seats, used for sports or entertainment

102 ***bet*** (page 54)
an agreement in which you risk money on what will happen in a game or race

103 ***charity*** (page 54)
an organization that gives money and help to people who need it

104 ***concert hall*** (page 57)
a building or large room that is used for concerts and other public events

105 ***published*** – *to publish something* (page 58)
to produce many copies of a book, magazine or newspaper for people to buy

106 ***imaginary*** (page 58)
not real, but only created in someone's mind

107 ***magic*** (page 58)
a mysterious power that makes impossible things happen if you do special actions or say special words

108 ***musical*** (page 59)
a play or film in which there are a lot of songs

109 ***classical music*** (page 60)
serious music that is played on instruments such as the piano and the violin. Someone who writes *classical music* is called a *composer*.

110 ***exhibition*** (page 61)
a public show where art or other interesting things are put on display so that people can go and look at them

111 ***broadcaster*** (page 62)
a company that *broadcasts*, or sends out, messages or programmes to be received by radios or TVs. TV and radio programmes are broadcast by different TV and radio companies on *stations* called *channels*. Other ways of receiving TV programmes include by *cable* – a system in which signals are sent through underground wires – and *satellite* – an object that is sent into space to travel around the Earth in order to receive and send information.

112 ***Royal Navy*** (page 65)
the part of the British armed forces that uses ships

113 ***funeral*** (page 66)
a ceremony that takes place after someone dies

114 ***courage*** (page 66)
the ability to do things that are dangerous, frightening or very difficult

115 ***moustache*** (page 67)
hair that grows above a man's mouth

116 ***hit*** (page 67)
a song that sells a very large number of copies of the recording

117 ***printing press*** (page 69)
a machine that is used for printing newspapers, books, etc

118 ***spin*** – *to spin something* (page 70)
to twist fibres into long, thin threads to make cloth

119 ***the World Wide Web*** (page 70)
all the websites that organizations have created on their computers for people to look at using the Internet

120 ***the digital revolution*** (page 70)
the many changes that are taking place in society because of new inventions based on computer *technology* – advanced scientific knowledge and the machines and equipment that are made using it

121 ***recycling*** – *to recycle something* (page 72)
to change waste materials such as newspapers and bottles so that they can be used again

# Useful Phrases

***took control of*** – *to take control of something* (page 8)
to get the power to make decisions about what happens in a place or situation

***went on strike*** – *to go on strike* (page 17)
to refuse to work for a period of time as a protest about your pay or conditions of work

***give something up*** – *to give something up* (page 24)
to stop doing something that you do regularly

# Exercises

## Welcome To England

**Which of these things does *Welcome To England* talk about? Tick the boxes.**

| | | | |
|---|---|---|---|
| food | ☐ | accents | ☐ |
| size | ✓ | money | ☐ |
| nationalities | ☐ | politics | ☐ |
| geography | ☐ | sport | ☐ |

## History: Old and modern

**Put the events in the order they happened.**

- **a** Industry started to grow during the Georgian period. ........
- **b** Henry the Eighth introduced a new form of the Christian religion. ........
- **c** After Edward died, Harold became the king. ........
- **d** Women were given the vote in the early part of the twentieth century. ........
- **e** William the Conqueror won the Battle of Hastings and became the king. ........
- **f** The Romans came to England. ..*1*..
- **g** Queen Victoria ruled the UK for 64 years. ........
- **h** The Second World War took place. ........
- **i** Christianity was introduced by the Romans. ........
- **j** Between one and two million people died from the Black Death in 1348. ........
- **k** Elizabeth the First was the queen until 1603. ........
- **l** At the end of the nineteenth century, new technology and education made life better for people. ........
- **m** Then the Anglo Saxons arrived and introduced seven areas controlled by kings. ........
- **n** Elizabeth the Second became the queen. ........
- **o** The Vikings fought with the Anglo Saxons and controlled part of England. ........

## Traditions

**Write an event from the box next to the words they are connected to.**

~~Christmas~~ Easter Guy Fawkes Night Halloween
New Year's Eve Remembrance Day Shrove Tuesday

1 *Christmas* turkey, family and friends
2 ........................ resolutions, fireworks
3 ........................ pancakes, races
4 ........................ eggs, rabbits
5 ........................ witches, sweets
6 ........................ bonfires, fireworks
7 ........................ silence, red flowers

## Places

**Match a place 1–14 to what it is famous for a–n.**

| | | | |
|---|---|---|---|
| 1 | Stratford-Upon-Avon | a | the government |
| 2 | Newquay | b | the Ashmolean |
| 3 | the New Forest | c | William Wordsworth |
| 4 | the Pennines | d | William Shakespeare |
| 5 | the Norfolk Broads | e | King's College |
| 6 | Cornwall | f | hunting and ponies |
| 7 | London | g | plates, cups and bowls |
| 8 | Bath | h | the Brontë sisters |
| 9 | Stonehenge | i | surfing |
| 10 | Oxford | k | the Royal Pavilion |
| 11 | Stoke-on-Trent | k | rivers and birds |
| 12 | Brighton | l | the Eden Project |
| 13 | Cambridge | m | baths and parks |
| 14 | the Lake District | n | a stone circle |

## Vocabulary: Nature

**Match a word from the box to its definition.**

coves   hedges   hunting   moorland   trails   waves   ~~wildlife~~

1 England has many different types of natural environments, so there are many types of animals and plants. ......*wildlife*......

2 The national parks are popular with visitors, who like walking along the small paths. ..................

3 Hundreds of years ago, the kings liked catching and killing animals in England's forests. ..................

4 Many of the small country roads have trees that grow close together on each side. ..................

5 Where the land meets the sea, there are many small areas to go surfing.

..................

6 The surface of the sea, especially in the wind. ..................

7 People also like walking on high land, which is covered with grass and plants. ..................

## Vocabulary: Famous people

**Match the people 1–8 to their descriptions a–h.**

| | | | |
|---|---|---|---|
| 1 | Horatio Nelson | a | wrote plays for the theatre |
| 2 | Charles Darwin | b | was a scientist and studied gravity |
| 3 | Sir Isaac Newton | c | was a scientist and studied animals and plants |
| 4 | Winston Churchill | d | stopped the French from invading Britain in a famous battle |
| 5 | Shakespeare | e | stopped the Spanish from coming to England by sea |
| 6 | Charlie Chaplin | f | was the prime minister during the Second World War |
| 7 | Margaret Thatcher | g | was the prime minister during the 1980s |
| 8 | Sir Francis Drake | h | was a popular actor in silent films |

## Vocabulary: Battles

**Complete the gaps. Use each word in the box once.**

allies battles bombs empire independent
~~invaded~~ power societies swords weapons

1 People from different countries ......*invaded*...... England because they wanted to live there and control it.

2 The people tried to organize .................................., in which people lived together and followed laws.

3 However, a lot of people died fighting in .................................. .

4 Each side wanted to have .................................. and control the country.

5 They used .................................. to kill each other.

6 A long time ago, they used .................................., which were like very big knives.

7 Later, .................................. were used, and these caused an explosion and fire when they hit something.

8 Sometimes, different countries agreed to fight together and became .................................. .

9 Britain also started to control other countries and formed an .................................. .

10 However, the countries were not happy and eventually became .................................. and had their own rulers.

## Vocabulary: Word building

**Complete the table with the correct form of the words. Then mark the stress on the words.**

| ADJECTIVE | NOUN |
|---|---|
| 1 independent | *independence* |
| 2 | power |
| 3 political | |
| 4 | competition |
| 5 imaginary | |
| 6 | education |
| 7 enthusiastic | |

**Complete the sentences with one of the words from the table.**

1 English people are very ............ about sport. They love it!

2 A ............ called jousting was very popular. Knights on horses showed their fighting skills.

3 America got ............ from England in 1783. They now had their own ruler.

4 In the twentieth century, women wanted more ............ power. They wanted to show their feelings about the government.

5 In the Georgian period, the government became more ............ than the king.

6 After 1944, children were more ............ because the schools were free.

7 The writer JK Rowling has a very good ............ .

## Vocabulary: Anagrams

**Write the letters in the correct order to make words which match the definitions.**

| | | | |
|---|---|---|---|
| 1 | LOCA | *coal* | something from underground which produces energy when you burn it |
| 2 | YENCRES | | the natural things you can see outside |
| 3 | LUFE | | a general word for things that produce energy; gas, for example |
| 4 | SHIBURB | | things you don't want or need anymore because they are useless or old |
| 5 | RONI | | a dark, very hard metal used for making steel to build strong structures |
| 6 | CHEPES | | a formal talk given to a group of people |
| 7 | TIMMIRANG | | a person who goes to live in a different country permanently |
| 8 | RAGEOUC | | the ability to do dangerous things |
| 9 | TROP | | the area where ships stop in a city |
| 10 | GIMAC | | this makes impossible things happen by saying or doing special things |
| 11 | TUREARETIL | | poems, stories or plays which are special and artistic |
| 12 | STULCRUPE | | a piece of art which is made from stone, metal or wood |
| 13 | DUM | | soft, wet earth |
| 14 | CHARM | | when people walk together to complain about something, often political |

**All the words above are nouns. Find nine uncountable nouns.**

## Grammar: Articles

**Complete the sentences with *a/an*, *the* or nothing.**

1 Every year the Queen gives ..*a*.. speech to the country.

2 Many people watch .......... Queen's speech on TV.

3 *Another Place*, in Liverpool, was built from .......... iron.

4 Sometimes .......... immigrants had problems in the UK.

5 England has .......... wonderful scenery.

6 Winston Churchill talked about having .......... courage.

7 The *Harry Potter* novels are about .......... magic.

8 The oldest houses in England were made from .......... mud.

9 Thousands of people went on .......... march through central London in 1990.

## Grammar: Correct the mistakes

**Every sentence contains a mistake. Underline the mistake and write the correction.**

1 Many school student wear a uniform. ........*students*........

2 Children must to go to school until they are sixteen. ..............................

3 People really enjoy to watch sport on TV. ..............................

4 Thousands of people are running in the London Marathon every year.
..............................

5 One of England's most famous writers is Shakespeare, what wrote *Romeo and Juliet.* ..............................

6 Fred Perry was winning Wimbledon three times. ..............................

7 Alfred Hitchcock borned in England. ..............................

8 English persons watch about twenty-five hours of TV a week.
..............................

9 Robin Hood has lived in Sherwood Forest. ..............................

10 England have many different types of heroes. ..............................

11 The city is busier the countryside. ..............................

12 We have had the World Wide Web for 1990. ..................................

13 Today, the Word Wide Web is change many things. ..................................

14 We has known about environmental problems for a long time.

..................................

## Making Questions

**Write the questions for these answers.**

1 The Beatles came from Liverpool.
Where ..........*did The Beatles come from*.......... ?

2 The UK joined the European Union in 1973.
When .................................................................... ?

3 English people go to the pub or the cinema at the weekend.
Where .................................................................... ?

4 They usually eat at home.
Where .................................................................... ?

5 The Romans built Hadrian's Wall between England and Scotland.
What .................................................................... ?

6 William the Conqueror came from France.
Where .................................................................... ?

7 Queen Elizabeth the First died in 1603.
When .................................................................... ?

8 People eat pancakes on Shrove Tuesday.
What .................................................................... ?

9 The Queen goes to the Houses of Parliament every November.
Where .................................................................... ?

Macmillan Education
4 Crinan Street, London, N1 9XW
A division of Springer Nature Limited
Companies and representatives throughout the world

ISBN 978-1-3800-4172-2
ISBN 978-1-3800-4107-4 (with CD edition)


Written by Rachel Bladon
The author has asserted her right to be identified as the author of this work in accordance with the Copyright, Design and Patents Act 1988.

First published 2013
This edition published 2019



Designed by Carolyn Gibson
Map (p4) by Peter Harper
Cover photographs by Alamy/Brian Jackson (tl), Superstock/Loop Images (r), Superstock/Steve Vidler (bl).

The author and publishers would like to thank the following for permission to reproduce their photographs:
**Alamy**/M.Abrahams p59, Alamy/Aflo Co Ltd p29, Alamy/amc p20, Alamy/A.Copson/City Pictures p57, Alamy/K. Grzymajlo p63, Alamy/Interfoto p60, Alamy/D.Levenson p26, Alamy/P.Ridsdale p53, Alamy/picturesbyrob p51, Alamy/P.Ridsdale p53, Alamy/Skyscan Photolibrary p66, Alamy/Superstock p7, Alamy/N.Tingle p52, Alamy Stock Photo/Trinity Mirror/Mirrorpix p18(t), Alamy Stock Photo/travelbild p42; **Bananastock** pp24(tr), 47; **The Bridgeman Art Library** /'The Wealth of England: the Bessemer Process of Making Steel', 1895 (oil on canvas), Titcomb, William Holt Yates (1858-1930) / Kelham Island Industrial Museum, Sheffield, UK p15; **Corbis** pp40(shark), Corbis/FLPA/P.Reynolds p40(pony), Corbis/B. Lewis/In Pictures p22, Corbis/Maskot p49(bl), Corbis/Design Pics/C.Tuttle p49(cm), Corbis/S. Zankl/Visuals Unlimited p40(porpoise); **Digital Vision** p40(fox); **Eyewire** p40(eagle); **Frank Lane Picture Library**/S.Hunter p40(badger), Frank Lane Picture library/S.Litten p40(robin), Frank Lane Picture Library/M.Rose p40(otter); **Getty Images**/AWL Images pp1, 37, Getty Images/Photographers Choice/Dominic Burke p16, Getty Images/ Photolibrary p28, Getty Images/RooM/AnjelikaGretskaia p24(br), Getty Images/Universal Images Group pp11, 64, Getty Images News pp70, 71; **Hulton Archive** p17; **Hulton Royals Collection** p68; **Image Source** pp31, 36, 40(hedgehog); **John Foxx Images** p40(squirrel); **Macmillan Australia**/Ian Faulkner p4; **Macmillan Publishers Ltd**/R.Judges p43; **Photographers Choice** p30; **Photofusion**/U. Klaphake p46; **Photodisc** p40(rabbit), 40(deer), 40(seal), 40(butterfly), 40(bat), 40(puffin); **Pixtal** recurring image on every page (phone box); **Rex Features**/J.Curtis p44, Rex Features/R.Hallam pp6, 27, Rex Features/Snap p62, Rex Features/W. King p55; **Stockbyte** p5; **Superstock**/Robert Harding Picture Library pp10, 33, Superstock/Loop Images p72, Superstock/Science & Society p69, Superstock/Stockbroker p23, Superstock/P. Thompson/Prisma p35; **The Image Bank** p39; **Wire Image** p21, Westend61 p18(inset).



Printed and bound in Great Britain
by Bell & Bain Ltd, Glasgow

without CD edition
2023 2022 2021 2020 2019
10 9 8 7 6 5 4 3 2 1

with CD edition
2023 2022 2021 2020 2019
10 9 8 7 6 5 4 3 2 1